D0342318

ALSO BY LAWRENCE JOSEPH

Shouting at No One (1983)

Curriculum Vitae (1988)

Before Our Eyes (1993)

Lawyerland

WHAT LAWYERS TALK ABOUT WHEN THEY TALK ABOUT LAW

Lawyerland

LAWRENCE JOSEPH

Farrar, Straus & Giroux / New York

ⵣⵣⵛⵛⴰ

Farrar, Straus and Giroux
19 Union Square West, New York 10003

Published simultaneously in Canada by HarperCollinsCanadaLtd
Printed in the United States of America

Designed by Abby Kagan

First edition, 1997

Library of Congress Cataloging-in-Publication Data
Joseph, Lawrence, 1948–
    Lawyerland / Lawrence Joseph. — 1st ed.
        p.   cm.
    ISBN 0-374-18417-8 (hard : alk. paper)
    1. Practice of law—New York (State)—New York.
    2. Lawyers—New York (State)—New York.   I. Title.
    KF297.J64   1997
    349.73'092'2—dc21   97-905

Frontispiece: Le Défenseur (For the Defense),
by Honoré Daumier, early 1860s, courtesy
of the Phillips Collection, Washington, D.C.

FOR JOSEPH JOSEPH

Contents

A NOTE TO THE READER

This is a work of nonfiction. It consists of exchanges among lawyers about law and lawyers, and, in many instances, the names, circumstances, and characteristics of the persons and places portrayed have been changed. In Joseph Mitchell's words—in his Author's Note to *Old Mr. Flood*—*Lawyerland* is truthful rather than factual, but solidly based on facts. There was no other way to write it. Those readers who are also lawyers will especially appreciate why.

*Don't be confused by surfaces; in the depths
everything becomes law.*

—RAINER MARIA RILKE

Robinson's Metamorphosis

L ET ME SEE. LAWYERS." ROBINSON TURNED HIS chair around with his body and pulled a file off the shelf, then, swinging back, tossed a newspaper clipping across his desk. "Here"—he smiled— "you want lawyers? Here's a lawyer. A white shoe, metamerger, 'don't-you-love-the-Four-Seasons-Grill-Room?' attorney-at-law. In a state of lament. He's lamenting! What is he lamenting? The demise. Of what? The profession. The profession! Why? Greed. That's what he says—greed! Two wives, four cars, three houses, two precociously gifted Ivy League children, driven to and from work down Park Avenue every day in a stretch limousine by some greasy-looking Green Card, when, one sunny morning, our American Esquire awakens to—a vision! A veritable William Blake! In capital letters! LAWYERS AND

GREED! Lawyers and greed! And you watch! Guaranteed! On the Op-Ed page of the paper of record. His visions will multiply! LAWYERS AND—God, whatever happened to—COMMON SENSE! LAWYERS WHO—can you believe it?—SCREW THEIR CLIENTS! LAWYERS AND JUSTICE! Justice!"

"You keep a file on lawyers?" I asked. Robinson laughed. Then, with an unsettling quickness, his whole demeanor changed. His face grew long, his eyes softened, his body slumped. I'd noticed this kind of transformation in lawyers before.

"Here's another one," he said. "The Attorney Fucking—or, I should say, the Fucking Attorney—General of the United States. In a talk to the American Bar Association, she tells them she loves them. Loves them! I do believe"—Robinson's voice quickened—"I love them, too! I am one, after all, now aren't I? And do you know what? What I think? I think America in its heart of hearts loves its lawyers. How can it not? Christ, there's one in nearly every family now! How can you help but love someone who knows how to drop the words 'emotional distress' into a conversation on the phone with some moron who's telling him the computer says he's not going to get the full amount of health insurance for the breast-cancer test his wife really didn't have to have, when—presto!—three days later there's a check in the mail for the full amount, with a letter of apology from the Empire State Blue Cross supervisor who, no doubt, is a lawyer himself, because you have to be a lawyer these days to even qualify for the job?"

Robinson sat back, gazing silently from his office window onto Lafayette Street. We'd gotten together for lunch, which we hadn't done in over a year. We knew each other from law school—Michigan, the early seventies. Robinson's appearance hadn't changed that much. Of medium height, he was still thin and wiry, and still had a shock of unkempt black hair. His arctic-blue eyes were, if anything, set deeper in his face. Robinson was a bit of a law-school legend. He used to carry around novels like E. L. Doctorow's *The Book of Daniel* and Saul Bellow's *Mr. Sammler's Planet*, and subscribed to *The New York Times* and the *Financial Times* of London. He wore a long black leather coat—the kind Richard Roundtree wore in *Shaft*—and a wide-brimmed Borsalino. Drafted into the Army after graduating from Queens College, he'd seen action in Vietnam, rare among my classmates. When I asked him about it, he lectured me on—a phrase I still remember—"the reconciliation of freedom and the state." His full name was Oliver Robinson—well, actually, C. Oliver Robinson, though everyone called him Robinson. No one knew what the C. stood for. Once, in property class, after he was called on and replied that he wasn't prepared, the professor, who wasn't much older than we were, looked at the seating chart and said, "Robinson, C. Robinson. What's the C., Mr. Robinson?" Robinson shot back, "C., sir—C. As in C. C. Rider. You know, 'see what you have done.' " A finalist in the Moot Court competition, during oral argument he summarized a United States Supreme Court opinion written by Justice Byron "Whizzer" White, who, it so happened, was right there staring at him, a Moot Court judge. White, interrupting him, said, "Counselor, I think you've misstated the rule. In fact, I know you have. How do I know? Because I devised it.'' Without missing a beat, Robinson, stroking the goatee he wore back then, said, "I am, Your Honor, quite aware you devised it. But with all due respect, sir, I must say that your appreciation of the constitutional law from which you devised it was misplaced then, and—with all due respect, sir—it is misplaced now." Robinson then took a quick look at a portrait of Clarence Darrow—who went to the Law School—on the wall behind the Moot Court bench. White shook his head and grinned. The audience went wild.

While everyone was arguing about this or that, Robinson would wave his hand in dismissal. "It's crap," he'd say. "It's really quite simple. A real lawyer knows how to take care of a legal problem." He said it often—it was one of his maxims. After law school—this was seventy-five—Robinson returned to New York, not a popular spot then, the city on the edge of bankruptcy and all, to clerk for a federal judge in Brooklyn. He then worked as an assistant district attorney for New York County. "The technical designation for this, the—to quote the song—isle of joy, Manhattan," he'd say, laughing. After he took the job with the Manhattan D.A., I asked him why he wanted to be a prosecutor, which, I pointed out, involved putting people in jail. "Is that right?" he said mockingly. "I'm really glad you told me that. I hadn't realized that. Look," he went on, "at least I'll know how to try a case." In the early eighties, he left the D.A.'s office to work for the Securities and Exchange Commission in Manhattan. Then, after a short stint with the Federal Defender's office, he went out on his own. "I am a criminal lawyer," he once told me after I asked about his practice. "I trust," he added with sarcasm, "the double meaning doesn't escape you." He does most of his work in federal court now. "I'm actually quite a successful federal court litigator," he said. I asked about his clients. "My clients? None of your fucking business, my clients. But if you really must know, as a rule I shy away from clients with money enough to put me on a retainer. If you have a criminal problem, and enough cash to put me on retainer, chances are you just might be involved in—what does R.I.C.O. mean again? Chances are you might just be involved in a racketeer-influenced corrupt organization."

"So you don't do R.I.C.O.?"

"Did I say that?" asked Robinson. "I don't think that's what I said." He paused. "Look," he went on, his voice softer. "It's simple. I don't like being beholden to anyone. It's as simple as that. I've got my limits. That's all. I live perfectly fine within my limits. I pretty much choose my clients. If you do this shit for as long as I have, and you're not a dumb fuck—which I am not—and you're not pigged-out on cash—which I am not—you find a niche. I got my niche.

"I will be the first to admit, though"—he rolled a pencil between his palms—"this has become one fucking incredible business. Two Decembers ago, the winter before last, two Decembers ago—I don't think I ever told you this. This client of mine—I do not lie—a twenty-year-old son of Fujianese and Serbian immigrants. Half, from what I can figure out, Fujianese, and half, on his father's side, fucking Serbian! So whose abode does this young American decide to enter one dark and dreary December morn? Are you ready for this? The apartment of an Assistant United States Attorney for the Southern District of New York. The apartment of a federal prosecutor, a fucking D.A.!—and I don't mean duck's ass, either! Two o'clock, one December morning—it's freezing outside—this young citizen climbs up a fire escape and pries open what turns out to be the bedroom window of a federal fucking D.A., who happens to be in bed beside his wife, who happens to be an investment banker at one of the more renowned houses, their two-month-old baby daughter blissfully asleep in her crib. Suddenly our D.A. is awakened from his slumber by a noise at the window. There's a silhouette behind the Venetian blinds. What went through his mind?—what would go through the mind of any trained lawyer! Our D.A. has one of those new hand-sized automatics—licensed, of course—so he's not thinking about getting the fuck out of there or calling 911. He knows, as any good lawyer knows, he has the perfect civil right to kill this young American. But, as any ambitious assistant United States attorney would, he's also thinking what he ought to be thinking— about the kind of unfortunate publicity such an act would engender in the information capital of the world."

"You mean the kid . . ."

"It's exactly what I mean. Patience, will you? Please? Will you let me finish? So what does our federal D.A. do? He wakes his wife, calmly tells her to get the baby and go out into the hall, which she does. He gets his gun and waits beside the window. Our Sino-Serbian boy wonder begins his descent into the room when—lo and behold!—his hair is being pulled

out. I mean pulled out, literally, clumps of it, right
out of his head, which our D.A. takes into his hands
and beats several times against the wall. Don't
laugh," Robinson said. "It's not funny! I know! You
think our D.A. has a bit of pent-up rage?"

"How . . ."

"Patience!" Robinson said, tossing his pencil onto
his desk, an expression of mock irritation on his face.
"Will you let me finish? It gets better." He took a
quick breath and sighed. "Well, of course, our D.A.
has our boy arrested—et cetera, et cetera. One thing,
though, is absolutely clear. Our D.A. wants our young
American—well, to put it in the vernacular of the
street—dead. He quite simply wants him dead. But
as any officer of the court knows, when it concerns
you directly, you have to be particularly careful
about letting your personal feelings interfere with the
cause of justice, right? It turns out—coincidence!—
our federal D.A.'s brother-in-law is very high up in
the Manhattan D.A.'s office, my former place of em-
ploy. I know the guy. One of those street-smart blue-
bloods—a dying breed—who makes his living
protecting the commonwealth. The guy's good, too.
So he—blue-blood—gets the case assigned to one of
the best prosecutors in the office, a woman who's
better-looking and more charming than the best of the
male peacock jury ass-kissers, and twice as smart.
One formidable lawyer who very well knows how to
use everything to her advantage. Well, she does not
fuck around. She manages—this is before I come into
the picture—to get a grand jury to indict my boy on,
in descending, or ascending, order, depending on how
you look at it . . ."

Robinson stopped. "Oh, yes. I forgot to tell you. Our boy was also carrying one of these sleek, pretty eight-inch switchblades. With that little fact, this very sexy thirty-two-, thirty-three-year-old D.A. manages, with the assistance of testimony from her very credible Assistant United States Attorney witness, to seduce the grand jury into indicting our boy for—are you ready?" Robinson put his hand up, counting off five fingers as he spoke. "Attempted murder in the second degree, attempted robbery in the first degree, reckless-fucking-endangerment in the first degree, burglary in the first degree, criminal trespass in the first degree. Plus—I can't even remember them all— a slew of boilerplate offenses for concealing a deadly weapon.

"Well, after I inherit this—I don't even know what you'd call it—I, of course, want to plead. God, you should see this kid. *Dumb.* Not just dumb— *dumb.* Not one of the more intelligent among those who inhabit our criminal domain. He's got absolutely *no* clue. I mean, his home life is mainland Chinese and Serbian—his father is an accountant for some Pakistanis who run a limo service out on Roosevelt Avenue in Queens. The father actually has money. How? I know you're not ready for this—he plays the stock market! An investor in corporate equities! He hears about me from this . . . No"—Robinson laughed—"*that* I won't get into. The kid? He's not really a *bad* kid. A little hard to talk to, though. In fact, he doesn't talk—he more like grunts. Syllables. 'What happened?' 'Uh, uh, uh, uh.' There is *no* way I'm going to trial. But the prosecuting attorney, she's not thinking about a plea—she is thinking *blood.* She looks me in the eye and says with this soft, sexy voice that the People have every intention of going to trial. If that was all—but how about this? The kid's old man refuses to help his boy meet bail!"

Robinson shook his head. "I am *not* making this up. He says he wants to instill some character in him. That's what he tells me. He's had enough, he doesn't know what to do with the boy—he wants to make a man out of him, to teach him a lesson. He says he's Old Country—an Old Country Serb. His dream was for his son to go into the Army—he says that he realizes this little episode has probably nixed the boy's chances. What am I supposed to say—it doesn't look as if junior's ever going to make general? Well, of course, I try to talk him out of it. I tell him his son could be locked up for a while—but, no, he's insistent, he says he's tried everything with the boy, that some time in jail might scare him into becoming a solid citizen. So"—Robinson shrugged—"the kid ends up on Rikers Island, with more than ample opportunity to meet some of his more manly fellow citizens. Ever seen Rikers?"

"From a distance," I said.

"From a distance? From a distance! Have you ever been in a jail?"

"No."

"You've never been in a jail?" Robinson's eyes widened. "Really? You've never been in a jail? Fuck! Well, I wouldn't feel too bad about it—though, actually, I don't know why you *would* feel bad about it. I'm sure you're aware that our correctional facilities aren't among our most pleasant public places. Don't"—Robinson put his hand up—"say it! I know.

Why should they be? Well, no need to worry. Rikers? Nice place, Rikers. How would you describe it? How about, gangs of murderers, rapists, drug addicts, and machine-gun-toting police to boot—in one wondrous place. The digs ain't cheap, either—more expensive a night than the Plaza.

"Which reminds me," Robinson said. "Don't ask me why it reminds me, but it reminds me. A conversation I had last week with a federal prosecutor. I was dropping my usual 'fuck-this's' and 'fucking-that's,' when he says to me, 'I'd appreciate it if you wouldn't be so vulgar.' This piece of shit—he's, like, twenty-eight years old, some Harvard former Second Circuit clerk, whose daddy, who's a partner at Ellis Parkman, got him the job. The little twit interrupts me—he'd *appreciate* it if I wouldn't be so fucking vulgar. I live in a society where there are how many? Twenty thousand murders a year? That's two hundred thousand murders a decade! Two million murders a century. Now, that's not vulgar, is it? Do you know how many children every day are getting smacked to death? How many skulls are being fucking crushed? Not including, of course, all those neat little, quote unquote, nonviolent felonies committed by our sisters and brothers over here in the World Financial Center. I'm sitting there with this asshole, plea-bargaining for a client who's had his fingers cut off by one of his colleagues in crime—whom our Federal Bureau of Investigation has yet to arrest because, I'm sure, our finger-cutter is an informer, which . . ." Robinson put both his hands up. "Look! I'm a citizen. I'm not naïve. I understand. I realize, these

days, even the Department of Justice is required to
operate on a cost-benefit basis. I looked at this fuck-
head, George—that's his name, George. 'George,' I
said, 'I appreciate it. I appreciate your telling me.
You're right, George—absolutely fucking right. I'm
just a fucking vulgar guy.' "

Robinson paused. "Rikers," he said. "It's an island." He was smiling. "All these islands—Liberty,
Ellis, Governors, Roosevelt, Staten, Manhattan, Rikers. Rikers is the third largest, after Manhattan and
Staten. Population about twenty thousand, very few
of whom attended their high school proms. The largest jail in the United States. I bet you didn't know it
has its own bakery—croissants for breakfast! Its own
mental-health facility—free psychotherapy! A full-
time tailor—buttons sewed on for free! Your classmates stick razor blades up their asses so they'll have
access to a weapon if things get rough. During visiting
hours their girlfriends French kiss small balloons full
of heroin into their boyfriends' mouths. Creative,
huh? Balloons!"

Robinson stopped and sat back straight. He'd
been leaning his head forward over his desk, his
shoulders hunched over. His face was calm. "We
should get going soon," he said after taking a deep
breath. "Before we do, though"—he motioned toward the window—"come look at this." I edged my
way between a row of file cabinets and his desk.
"Right here," he said, pointing out a stone figure—
a young woman in a robe and veil, flying, her right
hand raised beside a scale of justice—near the entrance to one of the city's courts. Beneath her on

one side was a serpent, on the other side an infant child.

"I hope you like Chinese," Robinson said after I sat down again. "Because that is what we're having. There's a place I like on the corner of Bayard and the Bowery, New York Noodle Town." I said that I'd heard of it, that it was supposed to be quite good. "Superb," said Robinson. "Especially if you know how to order, which I know how to do. I read in a magazine—I don't remember where—a leading French chef hangs out there when he's in town. There's a park behind the Tombs—we'll eat outside."

Robinson sat silently, rearranging some items on his desk. On it were a totem-like wood carving, a picture of his wife—a welfare administrator in the city's Department of Human Resources—pictures of their two daughters, two Rolodexes, and a plastic container of sharpened pencils. He took two CDs—Van Morrison's *Enlightenment* and Tori Amos's *Little Earthquakes*—which had been on his desk, and placed them on top of one of the speakers of a small boom box on a small table. He then turned the air conditioner on full blast.

"The kid," I said. "He wasn't doing too well."

"No," Robinson said. He put his hand on his chin, shaking his head. "No, the kid wasn't doing too well."

The look on his face was tense. "Do you know what fucking amazes me?" he asked. "What simply fucking amazes me? How little anyone who isn't a lawyer really knows about what comes down. I am simply fucking amazed. They all watch their lawyer TV shows, read these shitty legal thrillers, like it's one big, suspenseful, meaningful endeavor—some intricate mystery with a hidden truth revealed at the end of the final chapter. They hate lawyers more than anyone else in the world—but law? Law! They love the fucking law! You see it in jurors' faces—even the most sophisticated and street-smart. They're not only intrigued—they're impressed! Reasonable doubt—they go fucking bananas! Just say the words and their eyes change. Most people have how many? one, maybe two, reasonable thoughts a day. But ask them if they have a reasonable doubt about, let's say, the one person they love most in this world, and you'll get this 'what-the-fuck-does-that-have-to-do-with-it?' look. The same thing with intent. Mens-fuckin'-rea! God, how jurors love mens-fucking-rea! Ask them, though, if they knowingly intended to commit one of their own secret little crimes, and they look at you like you're some kind of pervert!"

Robinson's voice was getting louder. "No fucking idea!" he said. "I've been reading this biography of Learned Hand. Now there, you must admit, was, all in all, one impressive manic depressive. On the bench how many years? Fifty? That famous line of his—dread. Something like, he'd dread a lawsuit more than anything else in the world except dying. Fuhucking A! Consider, for example, this happy thought—an action against you by the People of New York County. Sometimes I think I became a lawyer so I'd know what to do if one of New York City's finest—for whatever reason strikes his or her fancy—decided I'd violated the Penal Law. Can you imagine not being a lawyer and getting dragged into this shit? You believe—it doesn't matter who you are—the idealized crap, like, you're not going to get fucked over, when, suddenly, you're under arrest. Dread, brother—we are talking Kierk-e-fucking-gaardian *dread*! Why the secret? Why not just tell everyone? 'Every lawyer shall tell his or her client that becoming involved with the legal system is like three years of experimental chemotherapy, one hundred percent guaranteed not to work.' Put it in the Code of Professional Responsibility! Place it on the agenda of the next annual meeting of the City Bar! What do the med mal people call it? Informed consent. Every citizen has the right to be informed of the truth! Make it a constitutional amendment! The Hand Man postmodernized!''

"How about the kid?'' I asked.

"The kid.'' Robinson sighed. "Our definitely dumb, not really bad, fucked-up, felon-kid. Well . . .'' He took a breath and paused. "Well—how do I want to say this? The judge, it turns out, through various social circles, knows the foxy D.A. prosecuting the case, as well as our D.A. victim—so I let everyone know, in my own discreet way, that I know it, and that I'm not afraid to shoot major mouth. Our boy ended up doing close to a year. Fuck, it wasn't like the People didn't need the room—space, you know, is at a premium these days in our penal institutions. Supply and demand. When I used to take court-appointed cases, I had clients who *wanted* to do time. I don't know if you've heard of the phenomenon. It's proven quite troublesome for our social theorists on both the left and the right. The client's thinking, 'So, I do a little time—networking time. Beats the streets.' Clients, brother—you know, not only your corporate clients lie. Clients down here in the nether regions know how to lie, too. Your client starts providing the prosecution with evidence that can be used against him—after a while you get the idea.''

"What do you do?''

"What do you mean, what do I do?'' Robinson stood up. "I do what I do. I'm Popeye the Sailor Man!'' He was laughing again.

"I do the Popeye, that's what I do. Remember? The dance! 'Pop, pop, Popeye, that's the name of the dance.' '' He was singing the song out loud. Meanwhile, stooped over, his body bobbing and weaving, head stuck out, he performed a series of alternating right- and left-hand salutes around his office.

We went out onto Lafayette Street—a hot, muggy July afternoon. Robinson left the jacket of his tan suit in his office, rolling up his white shirt sleeves and loosening his tie. "This way,'' he said. We crossed the street and walked through a small park next to the courthouse we'd seen from Robinson's window. Cardboard boxes, shopping carts filled with old clothes, food, bottles, newspapers—people were living there. At Centre Street we came to the sixteen-story-high, Art Deco–style Criminal Courts building, built by the federal Public Works Administration in the late thirties and early forties—two whole city blocks large. The first jail in Manhattan was located across the street on a site now a parking lot. Designed like an Egyptian mausoleum, it was known as the Tombs. The name stuck to the part of the Criminal Courts building that remained a jail. Robinson hunched over. "The *Tooooombs*," he said. "You probably don't remember—you never were into the criminal shit—when we were in Ann Arbor, sitting in Kamisar's Con Law class, the jail, which is on this side of the building"—Robinson pointed to his left—"was shut down. By order of a federal court. Said to have simply defied the human mind. Sealed cellblocks— virtually no ventilation. The noise was incredible—it fucking used to ricochet off the steel-and-tile surfaces. It's right in the court's opinion—a finding of fact— suicides, caused by the noise. There's also a description of the cellblocks at night—there was a sea of rats. A sea of wall-to-wall big fat gray jail rats!"

I asked if there was still a jail in the building. "Sure is," Robinson said. "Carpeting, air-conditioning, a rec room—state of the fucking art! Do you know what's also there? What will never change? What is forever? Besides"—Robinson broke into a smile—"the diamond in the front tooth of a client I once had? What even the most potent janitorial cleansers permitted pursuant to regulations promulgated by the Secretary of Labor under the Occupational Safety and Health Act will never get rid of? The *smell*. Years of accumulated, unwashed, human smell. Leftover piss-smell. It's still throughout the entire building. In the D.A.s' offices, which"—Robinson pointed to our right—"are over here, on this side of the building, and"—he pointed straight ahead—"in the courtrooms, which are here. A couple of which— the lobster shift—are open all night. Arraignments. You want to see a sorry-assed scene! Soda cans, coffee cups, potato chip, Dorito bags on the floor. The people, man! Jimmy Barnabooth—I've known him from way back when. He's in his fifties and still doing court-appointed lobster shift. I ran into him over on Hogan Place the other afternoon—he had on a checked tie, with pictures of Bugs Bunny in the little boxes. I was looking at it and Barnabooth laughed— he told me not to worry, that he wasn't in court that day. That's where you can still really smell the Tombs—the lobster shift. That damp, musty, almost puky smell—no question about it, it's still there. Any undertaker will tell you that you never get the smell completely out of a tomb.

"Look up there," said Robinson. The words EQUAL AND EXACT JUSTICE TO ALL MEN OF WHATEVER STATE OR PERSUASION. JEFFERSON were etched on the building's façade. "To all men—right on! Just a re- minder that our founders' original intent did not in- clude women. As for our Africano sisters and brothers—fuck, they didn't even count as 'whatever'! Not to deny, of course—like Martin Luther King once said—though the law ain't much for justice, at least it can stop lynching. You could legally lynch someone in several of these United States not even fifty years ago. Not anymore. In the early sixties California made it a crime to be addicted to a controlled substance. Unconstitutional. That you can't do. Today? Today"—Robinson shrugged—"the state of an un- due percentage of the persuasion of our citizens de- scended from our slaves is, simply, that they are poor."

We walked on Centre toward Canal Street. A woman came up to us, said "Immigration," and Rob- inson pointed downtown. "Do you know what this is?" he asked when we came to a passageway connecting the old Tombs with a new building. "The Bridge of Sighs. No, really, that's what it's called. Like in Venice. A bridge between the old jail and the new one—that's what this new building is—a new Tombs. It was a big controversy in the late eighties— what it would do to the neighborhood. How about this?" He pointed to a bas-relief of Buddha on the passageway. "Did you know Buddha has one hair between his eyebrows that sends out a constant buzz? Buuuzzzzz! Spiritual energy! Why are you laughing? You're such a fucking cretin. Of course, the more immediate reason for this bit of spiritual iconography is that the new Tombs is—like the old one—part of Chinatown."

We walked under the passageway over to Baxter Street, then several blocks to New York Noodle Town. Robinson recommended one dish of eggplant stuffed with fish, the shredded roast duck with garlic chives, and a rice dish with Chinese sausage and broccoli. We waited for our order at the side of the cash register. "Illegal," Robinson said in a near-whisper, with a quick nod toward a boy in his late teens sitting at a table across from us, his hair matted, his eyes darting back and forth, wearing a Harvard College T-shirt. "How can you tell?" I asked. "Fear," said Robinson. "Look at him. He's in a chronic state of terror."

We got our food and walked on Bayard to Columbus Park, which we'd passed on our way to the restaurant. We found a table of sorts—a slab of concrete, with chess and backgammon boards in colored stone embedded in its surface. There were benches on each side, which Robinson covered with napkins before we sat down. Most of the nearby tables were occupied by Chinese women, bags of food and vegetables beside them. Some were playing cards. "Look," Robinson said, "over there." He tilted his head toward the Tombs. "Human beings detained—isn't that a wonderful word, detained?—detained there right now. Someone right now may be looking out a window and watching us eat this outstanding—the Chinese sausage is delectable, isn't it?—haute cuisine. So might"—he nodded at the other side of the Criminal Courts building—"some A.D.-fucking-A. Over here," he said. He looked toward the new United States courthouse, some twenty stories high, on the south side of the park. "Cherrywood-lined elevators, white Vermont marble courtrooms, private kitchenettes and showers, brass doorknobs. Power—as we used to say—to the people. How is that for social space?"

"You know," I said, "I've never been able to figure you criminal-law types out."

"Figure this," Robinson said, lifting his middle finger.

"Seriously," I said. "It's not only that you're always around crime, which is one thing. But you're always around criminals. No matter which side you're on."

"We're always around police," Robinson said. He was sweating. "What you don't realize . . ."

He stopped. "Do you know what?" He took a handkerchief from his breast pocket, unfolded it, wiped his face, then, refolding it, carefully put it back. "The fuck if I know. I don't know if there is anything to figure out. Some deep personal pathology, maybe. Maybe something to do with my father. Or maybe it's just some deep need to get as close as I can to the whole thing. To the essence of the *thang*. The essence of the"—he smiled—"th*aaaang*. I can't remember where I saw it. Somewhere along the way. 'The criminal law represents civilization's pathology.' If you ask me, that's what should be written across the front of the Tombs. Tattooed on your Buddha! Maybe I'm just trying to figure civilization out. A noble purpose, after all!"

"What are murderers like?" I asked.

Robinson started to laugh. "Well, I've known a few."

"No, really. What are they like?"

"What do you mean, really, what are they like? What the fuck do you think they're like? They're insane, that's what they're like. It doesn't take too much to figure that out, does it? Premeditated murder. The idea of forming the intent to kill another human being—not in self-defense, not in war, which is a form of collective self-defense—it implies, doesn't it, that the mind of the murderer is capable of human thought, of human feeling? Doesn't it? But is anyone with a mind capable of human thought, of human feeling, capable of forming the intent to kill anyone? If you answer yes, what happens to our—what? Civilization? Our idealized sense of what makes us human? Look. Don't kid yourself. When we put people who murder other people in prisons—where, believe me, many of them, indeed, do belong—we don't do it because they're sane. We do it for other reasons."

Robinson wiped the sweat off his face with his

hand. "So what else do you want to know about murderers?"

I didn't answer.

"Well," Robinson went on, "I'll tell you something else about murderers. You know what about murderers? There's always an explanation. Always a reason why."

He stopped again. He seemed to be having trouble breathing. "Are you all right?" I asked.

"No," he said. He took a deep breath. "I'm going to stroke out on you, right here. Ruin your afternoon even more than I already have. Murderers!" He paused. "Murderers. A pleasant topic of discussion. You want to know the truth?—I try not to make it a personal thing. When I was with the defenders' office, years ago, there was a lawyer—this guy was really good, I respected him a great deal—I asked him how he dealt with rapists. To be honest, I've never particularly cared for rapists. In fact, I don't particularly care for human beings who torture, who enjoy torturing, other human beings. This person I asked —he's one of the most conscientious human beings I've ever met—says to me, 'Some of the kindest people I've ever known are rapists, and some of the most despicable animals on the face of the earth are rapists.' Pithy, no? Well, I've never forgotten it."

"You have to think about crime all the time."

"Never!" Robinson laughed. "But probably less than you think," he added. "Or probably more than I think." He stopped and continued eating. "Damn! This is the best roast duck in Chinatown, if you ask me. I can tell you this, though"—he swallowed a spoonful of rice—"not that it matters, but I will say this. It's its own thing. Do you understand what I'm saying? Crime. It's its own thing. Its own nature. And it changes, too. I will be the first to admit that things have gotten increasingly bizarre. I had a client who claimed he couldn't show up for a hearing because he had bubonic plague. Put that in an affidavit! And guns. Uzis, for example. Do you know what an Uzi is? It's a fucking submachine gun. You ask the resident surgeons in the emergency O.R. at Bellevue, they'll tell you about health care—the health care of machine guns. A twelve-year-old, who's not all there to begin with—add a hot temper and his own private Uzi. Nice! Plus the fact everyone in the whole damn society thinks they're watching themselves on TV or on a VCR—it doesn't matter who you are, what your purported ideology is. TV, video—they're sustenance. For the poor, for those of us who aren't poor—everybody's got to have it! It doesn't take a genius to figure out that if you're criminally disposed, and your mind's eye has turned into a moving camera, the human and inhuman intensity, the involvement in an act of physical violence, just might turn out differently than it used to—that a different kind of social sense is involved, or has evolved. Or look at it this way. Can civilization's pathology—our criminal law, remember—keep up with the pathology of our criminals? Have you ever wondered which pathology will prevail, have you ever felt that what we're really in is a war of . . ."

Robinson leaned back, taking several quick breaths. "God," he said, "I'm hyperventilating again." He sat for a moment. "I'm sorry," he said, shaking his head. "I'm probably not making much sense." He stood up, gathered together the empty food containers, and threw them into a trash bin. We started back to his office.

The afternoon air had turned into solid heat. We walked past the federal courthouse, then around to Foley Square. "I recently came across a book, *Conversations with Kafka*, by the son of a colleague of Franz's," Robinson said. "Do you know what Kafka did for a living? Workers' comp! It's true! He worked for the Bohemian Workers' Compensation Bureau. One of the first places there was workers' comp, in fact. Bismarck initiated it back in the eighteen-eighties. Today Kafka would be one of those lawyers —I mentioned that he was a lawyer, didn't I?—who works for a state department of labor, overseeing the workers' comp system. That's what Kafka did. He wrote reports on factory conditions. Workers' lungs destroyed by silicon. He knew the system cold."

We'd walked through Tom Paine Park and were standing at the corner of Worth and Lafayette. "You know what I realized?" Robinson asked. "I never really cared that much for Kafka. Admired, yes—but liked? Really liked? Never, really. Too much dream-like fantasy crap for my taste. Too imprecise. But in the middle of this not uninteresting book, Franz tells this young sycophant—or this young sycophant remembers Kafka telling him—'I am, after all, a lawyer. I am never far from evil.' Right-fucking-on, heh? I have to admit that I've always liked 'The Metamorphosis.' At least the idea of it. A guy gets up one morning from a night of horrendous dreams and finds himself changed in his bed into some kind of monstrous vermin.''

''A cockroach.''

''I don't think it's ever made clear—it's Kafka, remember? Vermin, monstrous vermin—you know, like in those landlord-tenant cases. The implied covenant of habitability and all that crap. What degree of vermin—aren't there degrees of vermin you need before you can get a constructive eviction? Well,'' said Robinson—we'd crossed Worth and were walking on Lafayette—''although you didn't ask, metamorphosis has always intrigued me.''

''Your own?''

''My own what?''

''Your own metamorphosis.''

''If the question is, yes or no, have I ever thought about my own metamorphosis, the answer is no. Except at one point I was tracking what you might call a more collective metamorphosis.''

''Collective?''

''You could call it that. There was a point I was watching it but could never determine when exactly it was. When the number of lawyers and the number incarcerated in every prison and jail in the country —federal, state, municipal—was the same. I kept a file on it. I thought when the numbers matched up it might be a nice switch. Every lawyer metamorphosed into a prisoner, every prisoner into a lawyer.

''Well,'' Robinson said, ''it went right past me. The numbers, I mean. Incarceration just took off. It's not even close anymore. We've got now—you'd be surprised, no one really knows the exact number—

somewhere between nine hundred thousand and a million lawyers, up around fifty thousand a year. Prisoners? Out of fucking sight! A million six and counting—a hundred-thousand-or-so increase a year. It's a major growth industry. It's why my business has been so good.''

We were approaching Robinson's building—we were in front of the windowless block-long black granite Manhattan Family Court building—when a slender young woman called out from the other side of Lafayette, then dashed across the street and greeted Robinson with a kiss on the cheek. Robinson introduced us, then turned aside, talking with her intensely. ''Nice to meet you,'' she said to me, moving her hand through her short sandy-colored hair. She then kissed Robinson again and ran against the light back across Lafayette. ''A beautiful woman,'' Robinson said. ''A federal defender. She's still learning how profoundly fucked-up it is. You have to learn the delay game—she hasn't yet learned how to be patient. She's got this fucking informant drug-dealing case. I don't do drug cases anymore. Not if I can help it. No fucking more.

''Well, anyway''—Robinson grinned—''the collective metamorphosis. The numbers weren't right. So I rethought it. Why not, if you're a lawyer, then you metamorphose into a prisoner, and if you're a prisoner, then you metamorphose into a lawyer. A tax lawyer in Washington, D.C., wakes up after a night of weird, nasty dreams and finds himself in an Arkansas penitentiary. He's there the next God-knows-how-many years for second-degree attempted arson—he fucked up trying to set fire to an empty apartment building. You go to sleep in your jail cell in Odessa, Texas, waiting to be arraigned for auto theft, and wake up, after the most horrendous nightmares of your life, a lawyer representing a body-piercing operation in Escondido—you know, outside San Diego—two hours before you've got a deposition, for which you're not at all prepared, in a malpractice case. One of your client's employees didn't properly disinfect one of those jeweled barbells—a twenty-year-old girl's nasal membrane is permanently damaged. Get the idea?"

"You realize," I said, "that you'd be increasing the number of lawyers."

"I hadn't thought of that," Robinson said. "Come to think of it, you'd be decreasing the number of prisoners, too. You always could, of course, metamorphose them back—status quo ante. What's wrong with that?" he asked. He took out his handkerchief and wiped the sweat from his forehead. "Lawyer becomes prisoner, prisoner lawyer—metamorphosed back into who you were. A form of exact—maybe exacting would be a better word—justice, that's all it would be," he said, his eyes squinting from the glare of the sun. "No more than a form of exacting justice."

Something Split

REALLY DON'T CARE," CARL WYLIE SAID AFTER I
asked him what he thought law was.

"Do you know what Holmes said it was?" I
asked.

"What did Holmes say it was?"

"A great anthropological document."

"A great anthropological document. A great anthropological document. What? The millions of tons
of paper generated every year by public offerings?
The billions of words written by lawyers every day?
How about the Supreme Court? That opinion declar-
ing unconstitutional that Colorado law—that one ap-
proved by a statewide referendum, by fifty-four
percent of those voting. The one that says no pref-
erential treatment for queers, no legislation privileg-
ing queers. I haven't read—I am never going to read

it, are you? Who ever reads Supreme Court opinions? I know I don't. It's like when a friend of mine from college asked me what I thought money was. I told him I didn't know and didn't really care. He said it's a social institution. Now, that says a lot, doesn't it? Money is a social institution. Chaos. That's what interests me. Chaos. What did Holmes say about chaos?''

''Chaos?''

''Complexity so intricate no one can fathom it. Large things within small things, small things within large things—things encompassing things which would seem to be beyond them. Chaos. Pardon me a minute, will you?''

Wylie walked over to the other side of the bar to make a telephone call. We were seated at a window table at Spartina, a bistro on Greenwich, a few blocks north of Chambers Street in TriBeCa. It was six o'clock, a warm, sunny September day. I'd known Wylie since the early eighties. He was lead partner on a multi-district bankruptcy securities fraud case I worked on when I was an associate with Sebold Manning & Pickering, a large New York firm. Because I'd been out of law school several years already when I came to Sebold Manning, I was only a couple of years younger than Wylie. Bulky, broad-shouldered, an avid tennis player, hair combed back tightly, graying on the sides, a bit long in the back, Wylie managed to make his presence felt. As he talked, he'd move his body around in his chair, making quick motions with his hands, often impatiently. Before I arrived he'd ordered a glass of Chilean Merlot and a double espresso, and a pitcher of ice water. "I drink three, four of them a day," he'd told me, twisting a slice of lemon peel into his espresso, stirring it slowly with a white plastic straw. "Espresso and, when I'm at the office, chilled Volvic. During the day I try to eat only fruit. I can't even drink regular coffee, of any kind, anymore—it has to be espresso. I time when it hits— the extent to which it speeds the thought process. That precise point when consciousness is heightened and everything glows."

Wylie returned, took a quick sip of Merlot, then sat back in his chair and relaxed, crossing his legs. "Busy," he said, shrugging, when I asked how he'd been. "The last few weeks in particular. My senior associate—we've been working on the Productive Data takeover. We represent one of the banks, a British bank—well, not quite. British banking laws are highly idiosyncratic. My associate—her name's Karen Tierney—she's excellent. She's definitely going to make partner. She's eight months pregnant. We've been working on this for months, there've been threats of litigation, all sorts of fighting—you may have read about it in the papers. It heats up again right after Labor Day—suddenly everyone wants the deal done. I'm back one day, after two weeks in the country. I am terrified Karen's going to miscarry. The other associate—nice kid—he's in his sixth year, tries hard, but just can't cut it. But I'm getting off-track. What I was saying. Every once in a while I don't think it's a bad idea for lawyers to remember that what goes on, at least on some level of our brains, is that we have to imagine everything coming apart. That's all.

No big deal. The Boy Scout motto—be prepared, right? It's what we are. Out of control, always prepared, Boy Scout control freaks."

Wylie took another sip of wine. "The other day I was sitting in a meeting—you remember Joe Tanner, don't you? Tanner's latest thing is that half our maladies come from sitting too long. Of course, there are exceptions. Shumacher, for example."

"Didn't Shumacher leave?" I asked.

"Yes. Francis departed. Not, may I add, of his own volition. He's now head counsel for Olympus. Over a million a year. The weapons-procurement business. Armament transactions. I don't know, so don't ask me between whom! He owns a manor estate deep in the heart of Virginia. Breeds racehorses. It's what makes Shumacher exceptional—he's exceptional at meetings. Which goes to show that you can make a million dollars a year by pretending to know what you're doing, and being able to sit through interminable meetings without developing any serious maladies. Anyway, I was sitting in a horribly long and tedious one, and started thinking how many times I've gone through this kind of pressure—I mean of the four, five, six weeks, ten-, twelve-hour days, make-a-mistake-and-the-show-is-over variety. Let's see. Twenty-seven years, on average, say, four times a year—twenty-seven times four—one hundred eight. One hundred and eight times. Pressure's really not the right word for it, either. It's the *concentration*. That painful kind of fastidiousness, attentiveness. Details—how many details? Twenty-seven years—*trillions* of details! You ask me a month from now what the deal I've just done was about, I won't be able to tell you. Don't think it doesn't make me stop and wonder what it's done to my brain, either.''

Wylie uncrossed his legs and sat up in his chair, his elbows propped on the table. He poured himself a glass of ice water and slowly drank it. ''I made a remark to Whitney Fuller—he's in our Paris office now—about a lying bastard with Cronon Granby I'm trying to close a deal with. Fuller says, 'You've become a real cynic, haven't you?' What? I'm supposed to believe everything I hear? Cynical? Of course I am. How can you be a lawyer and not be cynical? But a cynic? I am not a cynic. Cynics are the second-, the third-raters. For the cynics I have nothing but contempt. There are rules, basic rules—they may change, they may or may not be to your liking—but there are rules. The cynics don't give a damn about the rules. Serious—well, serious I am. I take what I do very seriously. I happen to think it's a very serious business. Blood on the floor sometimes, right? Very seriously ironic—that's what. Nonlawyers think of lawyers and think corruption, arrogance, pretentiousness—all of which, more or less, of course, are true. But irony? If Schlegel's definition of irony were applied to the practitioners of our stately art, it'd be the end of the Republic.''

Wylie was smiling. ''Schlegel. The nineteenth-century German philosopher. Friedrich Schlegel. 'Irony is the awareness of the infinite plenitude of chaos.' Friedrich Schlegel.''

''Chaos,'' I said.

''Chaos,'' Wylie repeated, taking a sip of espresso and then of wine, sitting back again.

''Jeanne and I were at this dinner party Saturday

night up near the Guggenheim. Very wealthy people
—your hundred-million-dollar types. They had an
original Goya—a drawing. An absolutely beautiful
small Matisse, a large Cézanne, on one of their walls.
And these unbelievable American Indian blankets.
Our hosts—the wife is a friend of Jeanne's from
work, the husband a very nice guy, an anesthesiolo-
gist, the son of an Indiana glass family—glass as in
glass for automobiles. Of course there was another
lawyer there—there always is at least one. He was
about my age, a couple of years younger, maybe. The
first thing he asks—I hate it when another lawyer
does this to me at a purely social occasion—is what I
do. I tell him the firm. Oh, he says, he knows several
of my partners. Then he asks what my practice is.
Corporate, I say. He's waiting for me to ask him what
he does, but I'm not in the mood, so I just sit there
and don't say a word. So how's he break the silence?
He asks what law school I went to! Fordham, I say.''

"You went to Virginia."

"Who cares what law school I went to? Gary Pap-
pas is one of the best lawyers in our firm and he went
to Albany. What this guy wants me to know is where
he went to law school. I ask him. 'Yale,' he says. Of
course. Have you ever known anyone from Yale who
didn't let you know that he went to Yale? Well, as far
as I was concerned, that was enough chitchat with
Boola-boola. I knew what was coming next—Bill and
Hillary Clinton and Clarence Thomas stories. 'Those
wild, halcyon days at the'—ever notice that about
boolas? That it's always *the* Law School?

"Well, the evening, as it wound on, was, actually,
quite pleasant. There was a movie producer there,

and a vice president at ABC—*not* a pleasant business
these days—a younger woman who works at the
Rockefeller Foundation, a young man in advertising
who does a lot of work in Berlin—if you think things
are insane here, you should hear what's going on in
Berlin! There's the usual small talk, the wine is excellent, which always helps. Then, what always
happens—what you always end up talking about at
every dinner party, it doesn't matter where—crime.
Have you noticed? Everyone—even the otherwise
very quiet Polish women who clean our offices—has
crime on the brain. Of course, since we're lawyers
we're supposed to know more about it than anyone
else. So I tell my crime story. I'm walking back from
lunch at Arcadia—they've got that great lobster
club—when a flash of blue jeans and ponytail on Rol-
lerblades grabs a cellular phone right out of the hands
of a Japanese, and punches away, probably, as he
blades right up Park Avenue. In broad daylight, as
they say. Boola-boola then tells his. He lives on Madison in the upper Nineties—there've been armed rob-
beries right in front of his building. His solution?
Troops.''

''Troops?''

''Federal troops. The Eighty-second Airborne.
The paratroopers. On every corner. And camps.
Work camps. Put them all in work camps. 'Troops—
that's right—troops,' he says, while he's bringing this
fairly large piece of leg of lamb at the tip of his fork,
a bit of mint on it, up to his palate. And there these
other people are, listening to him intently, as if he
knows something they don't—except the young man
in advertising, the one who does business in Berlin.

He says, 'But wouldn't the presence of federal troops depreciate property values?' To which Boola, with utmost sincerity, says, 'That's a good point. I hadn't thought of that. I'll have to think about that.'

Wylie moved his shoulders around, then pulled back again in his chair. Sitting a moment in silence, he suddenly seemed restless. I asked how things were at the firm. "Things at the firm? Changing," he said, and then was quiet. I asked how. "How? More pressure to bring business in, for one thing. That's how. You don't keep up, you're irrelevant fast—real, real fast. Gene Sutton, you know, just retired. At sixty."

"At sixty?"

"With a full—and for Gene that means a very full—pension. At sixty-five it's mandatory. Some firms are talking about making it mandatory retirement at sixty."

"That means that you . . ."

"Anywhere between eight and thirteen years from now and I'm out of here, with a full pension. The trade-off is, to get there I've got to work—there's absolutely *no* comparison—much harder than partners of my stature worked when I began. The business is so large now—and it's getting larger. We've got offices in seventeen cities now, eleven foreign. We just opened an office in Bombay. We're looking for associates who speak Hindi. The game is changing as we speak. Then, of course, there are those things that never change."

"Like?"

"Like, what lawyers do is determined by our—by 'our' I mean by our clients'—interests. It doesn't matter what kind of practice you have. It's always been that way and always will be. What we do is determined by who pays us. There's not a whole lot more to it than that. How long does it take before you figure it out? Second year of law school? Conscious—conscientious—schizoids.'' Wylie's face broke into a grin. ''Conscious, or, if you're the ethical type, conscientious schizoids, that's what lawyers are. I can't tell you who,'' he continued, lowering his voice, ''but one of my partners—you know him—was in psychoanalysis. This, of course, is between me and you. Attorney-client.''

''He's your client?''

''You know what I mean. Attorney-client. If you tell anyone, I will simply annihilate you.''

''Who is it?'' I asked.

''Jack. We'll call him Jack.''

''It's Cameron, isn't it?''

''I'm not going to tell you who it is,'' Wylie said. ''Just remember this is attorney-client. I don't care who you think it is.''

He finished his espresso, and, slowly, his glass of wine. ''An Epicurean's upper-downer,'' he said with a quick shake of his head after he finished, then went on.

''Jack. Yes, Jack. Jack's psychoanalyst—not, by the way, one of those Psychoanalytic Institute sorts. He's a psychiatrist, an M.D. A nonlawyer fascinated by lawyers. His father was a partner at Broderick & Williams. Deputy secretary of something or other under Eisenhower. One of John Foster Dulles's closest friends. There was a big scandal, hush-hush, something to do with Batista, male prostitutes, little girls —Jack doesn't know all the facts. There's a lot of that going around these days—children of lawyers who want to know what Father was really about. Father was the remote, secretive type—well, what a surprise! Anyway, the guy's into it. He tells Jack that Jack is in a state of schizogenesis.''

Wylie laughed. ''I had no idea what it meant, either. Jack—lawyer that he is—looks it up. It's a biological term. Reproduction by fission. Fission, splitting—Jack's paying the guy several hundred dollars an hour—'more than I get,' is how Jack puts it —to hear that his lawyer self is constantly splitting, and that he's replicating the split in every area of his life.''

Wylie looked at the expression on my face. ''It's not funny,'' he said. ''Jack is a decent guy. *Very* highly respected. A terrific lawyer. Jack is all right. The poor guy's had a lot of trouble in his marriage. One of the last of the real gentlemen in this business. Soft-spoken. Radiates confidence. Women love him. He's fallen in love with a younger woman, a partner—I'm not sure, she could be of counsel—at that small international securities firm, Dennis Phillips's firm. She's Venezuelan, the daughter of the former ambassador to the United States. I think she's an American citizen now. She's divorced—her first husband was American. A very connected investment consultant here in New York—you do a Latin American deal, she knows the players. She has a daughter, a three-year-old. Jack's got a child with some kind of birth defect, and his eldest son has a serious drug problem—I mean very serious, like, heroin.''

Wylie smiled. ''So what do you think triggers the doctor's prognosis? Jack, during one of his sessions, said that because he's a lawyer he has to constantly split hairs. Isn't that perfect! So what does the mind doctor say? He tells Jack that, as a lawyer, he has to be capable of deep moral compromise. You have to do things, be part of things, you don't want to be part of. You have to pretend to be what you're not. Well, you can't argue with that. We all know there are times when you're working on some deal that, if you were to think it through, you'd realize that it was going to ruin the lives of thousands of people and their families. We all do it—in one size, shape, form, or other. According to the doctor, the split that occurs when we do this is subconscious. It has to be. If it weren't, we couldn't do it. This, for the doctor, is a big, big deal. He says that lawyers, when they do something they really don't want to do, end up subconsciously sublimating their real feelings into—well, money, of course, and success. Status, power, the fact that by being a lawyer you are satisfying your father and mother—that sort of thing. This is the trouble, the doctor says. Imagine, the doctor tells Jack, what happens is like a cesspool of poison. He actually tells Jack—who, by the way, has put together toxic-waste-dump deals!—he tells him to imagine his brain's got a toxic-waste dump in it! The poison in his brain is anger, which, psychologically, manifests itself in one of two ways—in violence against others, or in violence against oneself. The violence against oneself most often expresses itself in a form of depressive behavior, which includes drinking—which Jack does much more than he should. The violence against others . . .''

Wylie stopped. ''I know what you're thinking—psychobabble, right?''

"No, not at all," I said. "I always found Jack intriguing—though I'm not supposed to know who Jack is."

"Well," Wylie said, slumping back into his chair, arms folded, "Jack is telling me this at nine in the morning. Right before we have to go into an all-day meeting. We're working on the Multivision Systems merger—we represent a consortium of Asian banks and our clients are here from Hong Kong, from Tokyo. It's going to be a long day and we've been working very, very hard. This is a two-and-a-half-billion-dollar deal, which, even these days, is a considerable amount of money. Jack? He says he saw his analyst—an emergency session—the evening before, after work, late, ten o'clock. He starts telling me what happened. This is right before we go into the meeting. He says the doctor—who, according to Jack, didn't look too hot himself, his eyes were bloodshot, he had that wiped-out look—the mind doctor begins the special session by asking Jack what he thinks he's learned about himself these past few months in therapy. Jack, a bit puzzled by the question, thinks it over and says, slowly, that he supposes what he's learned is that he is either chronically depressed, or he's chronically acting out his depression by drinking, or he's chronically engaged in acts of violence against others—or, depending on the time of day, all the above. The doctor says, 'Yes! Yes!' as if he's Edison or someone saying 'Eureka!' 'Yes! Yes! That's right, Jack! Yes!' Then Jack says, after a bit more rumination, that it's his understanding, too, that this chronic state of depression—this manifested violence

—has a lot to do with the fact that he's a lawyer.
'Good.' the mind doctor says. 'Good! You see that! Wonderful!' Suddenly, Jack says—don't forget our clients, who have come halfway around the world to pay us several million dollars for our services, are waiting for us outside my office and, I suspect, beginning to get a little irritated—suddenly, Jack says, something inside him *snaps*.

"You know," Wylie said, "I'm sitting there, thinking to myself, God, if these people had any idea what we were doing with their time. Here I am at my desk, looking over Jack's shoulder at the Chrysler Building, and there's Jack, pacing back and forth across my office, with this tight-lipped grin on his face, snapping his fingers. '*Snaps!* Yes, *snaps! Snaps!*' Then he starts laughing—too loud, in fact, for my comfort. 'That's right, something inside me—yes, of course— *split*. Something *split*!' I tell him to get on with it— I'm beginning to laugh myself. Jack says that he looked straight at his quack—that's what he's calling him now, his quack—rubbing his eyes, shaking his head. 'Well, yes, doctor, that is what I do,' he says in this calm, deliberate voice. 'Yes, I am a lawyer. That is how I make my living, doctor. I make my living by committing acts of violence against myself and acts of violence against others.' The doctor doesn't know what to say. Jack goes on. 'May I ask you something, doctor?' The doctor, not quite sure what is happening, says, 'Yes, of course, you can, Jack, of course you can.' 'Let me get this straight, doctor,' Jack says. 'What you are saying, in effect, is that because I am a lawyer, I am a pathologue—that is what we're saying, isn't it, doctor?' Jack said he'd lowered his voice to a whisper—he was staring at the quack as hard as he could. 'Is that what we are saying, doctor? Well, if it is, then, doctor, please, I want you to tell me . . .'

"Jack then looks at me. He tells me not to worry. He assures me that he's fine. He tells me not to worry about the clients, either. 'Remember,' he says, 'we're putting at least two billion clean in their pockets in a way no one else in the world knows how to do quite as efficiently as we do.' 'I know you're fine,' I tell him. 'If I didn't think you were, I'd already have had you locked up in one of the empty conference rooms. I just want to know what happened.'

" 'What happened?' Jack said. 'Simple. Before I could ask the question, mid-sentence, this guy I've given over thirty thousand dollars to bolts from his chair and says—with my exact same tone of voice—that he refuses to sit there and be cross-examined by me. Then, while he's showing me to the door, he tells me that he never wants to see me again, and says, and not parenthetically either, that if I think his prognosis is wrong, then sue him for malpractice.' "

Wylie and I left Spartina and walked to West Street, where he caught a taxi. I continued farther downtown to the World Financial Center, where, at a small bar and restaurant on the Hudson, Steamers Landing, I met Matt Jansen, Shana Urquart, and Bill Voorhees, former associates of mine at Sebold Manning. Now in their late thirties, they, too, left the firm in the eighties. You reach Steamers Landing via a long esplanade that extends along the river toward New York Harbor. From it you can see Ellis Island, the Statue of Liberty, Staten Island, and—its green lights silhouetted in the distance—the Verrazano-Narrows Bridge. Voorhees, Jansen, and Urquart were sitting outdoors when I arrived, two bottles of champagne and an array of appetizers on the table. The evening sky was violet-blue. There was a trace of sea salt in the air, warm still, and a nearly full moon. Across the river two Jersey City office towers cast long red and bright white reflections on the ebony water. Near one of them was a large round neon clock, a billboard shaped like a red Colgate toothpaste box beside it.

"So Wylie declined to join us? Well, fuck him," Jansen said with a laugh. He'd gotten heavy, almost stiff, but his large blue eyes were lively and expressive, and his voice had an easiness about it. "I heard he was named one of the best lawyers in New York by *New York* magazine."

"That wasn't Wylie," said Urquart. "Harry Balog was the only one from Sebold Manning." She brushed her dark brown hair back from her forehead. Attractive in a way everyone noticed—which she was aware of and used to—she spoke in a low yet distinct voice, at odds with the constant gestures she made with her hands. "At least he wasn't an idiot. He also didn't need to let you know every time he saw you he wanted to fuck you."

"Lauren Cobb," Jansen said.

"Clitless!" Voorhees shouted. Six feet tall and solidly built, he spoke in a tone on the edge of sarcasm. "I can't believe you used to call her that," Urquart said. "Nor can I believe that you're calling her that now."

"No comment," Jansen declared, waving both hands back and forth in front of his smiling face.

"Clitless Cobb. The iguana," Voorhees said. "Slimy. Bulging eyes. Do you think female iguanas have clitorises?"

"Don't you think we ought to change the subject?" Jansen asked.

"You brought her up, I didn't," said Voorhees. "But—not to change the subject too much—what do you think Wylie is making these days? Seven-hundred-fifty?"

"More than that," said Jansen.

"He's not making much more than that," said Voorhees.

"It's still a very wealthy partnership," Jansen replied. "I'd say a million at least."

"What are you making these days?" asked Voorhees.

"What am I making these days?" Jansen shot back. "None of your business, Billy. Has anyone ever told you how crude a fucker you are?"

"You can't be doing too badly," said Voorhees.

"I have health insurance—at least I did the last time I looked," Jansen said. "I'm not a temp."

"There are, you know, lawyers who are," said Urquart.

"I'm not at the point of putting off settling a case rather than give up the fees, like a lot of people I know," Jansen continued. "I don't know about you, but it costs me a lot of money to live these days. Three quarters of a million it's going to cost me just to send my children through school."

"Less than what Wylie makes a year," said Voorhees.

Jansen laughed. "Less than what Wylie makes a year. More, though," he added, "than what those *grease*balls who hustle what comes in off a street like Nassau make. They *really* hate our asses."

"I hate your ass," said Voorhees, "and I'm your friend. Even the personal-injury 'zoids . . ."

" 'Zoids?' " asked Jansen. "What's a 'zoid?"

"Short for sleazoids. Even the personal-injury 'zoids who make a hell of a lot more than we do hate our asses. We at least have clients who actually pay us. Can you imagine your livelihood depending on how brain-dead a brain-dead baby is? There's a term I heard the other day—'a cancer misdiagnosis case.' 'Please, Lord, won't you send me a cancer misdiagnosis case!' "

"We are the ay-leet-ists," said Jansen.

"The what?" asked Voorhees.

"Don't you remember?" Jansen asked. "That's how Stone used to say it."

"Stone! What ever happened to that Negro?" asked Voorhees.

"Negro?" asked Urquart.

"Stone's done very well for himself," said Jansen. "Quite well, in fact."

"Is he still with Connor Lachaise?" asked Voorhees.

"I think so," said Jansen.

"They're still downtown, aren't they?" asked Voorhees.

"On Battery Park," Urquart said. "In the same building Parkman & Millay used to be in. Did you follow that? Now, that was scary!"

"I heard," Jansen said, "that the creditors have exhausted the liquidation and insurance pot and have begun going after partners' individual assets."

"Clients," Voorhees said. He was shaking his head. "That's what happened. Clients. The rainmakers walked. Bye-bye! It's become a freelance business, in essence—that's what it is. And how it's going to be, too, for at least the thirty or so more years we've got left in it. A law professor I know sent me an article by Richard Posner, which . . ."

"You mean 'Book-a-month Posner'?" asked Jansen.

"He's smarter than you are," Voorhees said. "I can see you trying to carry on an intelligent conversation with someone like Posner. There's a story—it may be apocryphal. Posner clerked for Brennan. Brennan said he'd met two geniuses in his life—William O. Douglas and Posner."

"Is Brennan still alive?" Urquart asked.

"I think so," Voorhees replied. "To tell you the truth, I'm not really sure. I do know he's not on the Supreme Court anymore. If he is alive, he must be close to ninety. Anyway, Posner's article is too long —law-review articles are all too long—but at least you can read most—not all, but most—of what he writes without wanting to projectile-vomit. He says the business always operated like a cartel and, until the sixties, into the seventies, things were more or less under control—there were fewer lawyers, no advertising, there was a sense of the profession, there was enough to go around. Then the market, with the baby boomers, opened up—more lawyers, advertising. Dial 1-800-LAWSUIT—have you seen those ads? I saw one at a bus stop out on the Island. There's been an astronomical increase in the number of lawsuits. It's a service business now. Other than the margins—government, which pays so shitty—that's what it is. Partnership isn't worth shit. You do business with a partner or an associate to the extent to which you get more from them than what you're giving. They start sucking too much off you and you're out of there— you start sucking too much off them and you're out of there, too. It's happening everywhere. The big firms, three, four, five years"—Voorhees waved his right hand up and down in a mocking motion—"bye-bye! I have a client who's studied Genghis Khan. Khan was the first to use freelance brigades."

"The Mongol?" asked Jansen. "You have fucking flipped your lid!"

"It's a military term," said Voorhees. "A unit of military organization. A group of fighters, but everyone's freelance—on his own. You go with the flow. Winner take all, losers—losers *lose*. These people are serious. This client—Cal Tech. Phi Beta Kappa. He's thirty-three years old and has made two—going on his third—separate fortunes in computers. He does *not* care for lawyers. You should hear him talk about the fatsos—he *despises* fatsos."

"Watch yourself," said Jansen. "I'm not doing that well with the girth myself."

"You'd be an exception, Matthew. You, he'd love. That pudgy charm of yours is irresistible. Nah. What gets him going more than the girth are faces. He'll point at a lawyer and say, 'Look how twisted, how soft, how *false*, his face is.' I, of course, am excepted. He said my face was the first thing he checked out."

"Sounds like you're in love with him," said Jansen.

"You know what he says?" Voorhees leaned forward, his voice suddenly intense. "Clients have figured it out, he says. You make money by not only downsizing employees but downsizing your lawyers' asses, too. He asked me how long lawyers thought it would take before everyone figured out you can hire in-house counsel cheap—people like us—to watch over what people like us are doing with your money. Hire in-house counsel who can do the work. He reminded me that a lot of clients are lawyers, too—more than you'd think. They just don't tell you they are, which figures—they're lawyers!"

"The woman who runs the exercise machine at the gym I go to is—I should say was—a lawyer," Urquart said. "She worked a couple of years with the Queens D.A."

"What's that noise?" asked Jansen.

From a distance we could hear the sound of a band becoming louder and louder, until a boat with a salsa band on it—people on the boat dancing to the music—passed by on the river. The music then receded, disappearing as the boat went up the Hudson.

"*What* the *fuck* was *that*?" asked Voorhees.

"The *Fidele*," said Urquart.

"Fidele?" he asked with a shout. "Who? Fidel Castro?"

"It's the name of the boat in Melville's *Confidence-Man*," Urquart said. "I just started reading it—I've only read the first few chapters. It's *very* strange. This one incident—there's a black beggar, a cripple, a freed slave, on a boat, the *Fidele*, on the Mississippi at St. Louis. Before the Civil War. His name is Black Guinea. He's kneeling on the deck, his head thrown back, his mouth wide open, Melville says, like an elephant waiting for tossed apples—that's the way he describes it. People throw coins into this man's mouth like they're pitching pennies. When he catches one, he jingles his tambourine.''

''I really have *no* idea what you're talking about,'' said Voorhees.

''It's a novel,'' Urquart said. ''*The Confidence-Man: His Masquerade*. Herman Melville. I started reading it after I read—I was rereading it, actually —'Bartleby the Scrivener.' ''

''You have time to read?'' asked Voorhees.

''I like to read,'' said Urquart. ''So I don't play golf.''

''I don't think I've ever read 'Bartleby the Scrivener,' '' said Jansen.

''You didn't read it in high school?'' asked Voorhees. ''It wasn't in your high school English book?''

''Scriveners copied official legal documents,'' Urquart continued. ''Like law clerks today. I think some of them may even have been lawyers. The person telling the story's a bond lawyer. The type, one of those silly people—I had to deal with one the other day, in fact—who come right out and tell you he's successful. His office is at number-dash—capital N, small o, period, for number, then a long dash—Wall Street. I love the dash, don't you? That's the way it's written in the story. Melville didn't want to say exactly where the office was. His father and brother, apparently, were lawyers. His brother's firm was located at 10 Wall.''

"Is 10 Wall still there?'' asked Jansen.

"No,'' said Urquart. "There's no such number anymore. A number 2—the old Bankers Trust building—and a number 14, but no number 10. Melville's father-in-law was a lawyer, too, you know. A very famous lawyer, in fact. He helped support Melville when his career fell apart. Lemuel Shaw.''

"Lemuel Shaw?'' Jansen exclaimed. "Never in my life did I expect to hear again the name Lemuel Shaw! Herman Melville's father-in-law? Goddamn!''

"Take it easy,'' said Voorhees. "What are you going to do, go into spasms?''

"It's one of the few things I remember from law school,'' said Jansen. "We had this professor who taught an opinion Shaw wrote for—I always have to get this right—the Supreme Judicial Court of the Commonwealth of Massachusetts. Shaw wrote an opinion that returned a fugitive slave—basically, on jurisdictional grounds—to his owner in one of the Southern states. Shaw was an ardent Abolitionist— which the professor made into a big race thing— which, of course, it was. Shaw was big money. Made himself mucho moola before ascending to the Commonwealth's highest bench. Banking, real estate—today's money, we're talking, easily, two, three mil a year.''

"Bartleby, Lemuel. Names you don't hear that much anymore,'' Voorhees said. "There's a girl—my guess, Puerto Rican—who serves coffee at the Au Bon Pain near my office. The name on her tag is Yesenia.''

"I remember now," Jansen said. "Isn't 'Bartleby' the story where the guy keeps saying 'I prefer not'?"

" 'I would prefer not to,' " Urquart said. "He keeps repeating it every time he's asked to do something he doesn't want to do, which becomes a serious problem for his benevolent employer—at least he thinks of himself as benevolent—who tries to get himself out of it. Bartleby ends up starving himself to death in the Tombs. At the end of the story, out of nowhere, the bond lawyer says he'd heard that before Bartleby came to work for him he was a clerk in the dead-letters department for the post office in Washington. Bartleby was fired when there was a change in—he doesn't say which—administrations. Do you know what I liked most about it?"

"The number-dash Wall Street?" asked Voorhees.

"That, too," Urquart said. "No. The obvious. The 'I would prefer not to.' "

"You're not going to get heavy on us, now, are you, Shana?" Jansen said.

"No, I'm not going to get heavy," Urquart said. "When we worked at number-dash Wall Street—Mallorn. Do you remember Mallorn?"

Jansen shook his head. "Mickey Mallorn!"

"Mallorn was it for me. I got assigned to—he was the senior associate—this horrendous real estate case. The client was this old-line real estate family, the Godwins, an old client. A *God*-awful case. Tons of documents, terrible minutiae—I don't know if I've ever told you this. We were plaintiffs—Brownwell Eliot was on the other side. I can't remember a thing about it—it had to do with the terms of a ground lease. A twenty-million-dollar case. Mallorn was in way, I mean way, over his head. He really didn't know what he was doing. He had me draft a stupid memorandum of law for a discovery motion. The entire strategy was idiotic. I wrote it and he sends it back to me with THIS IS UNACCEPTABLE! across the top. He calls me into his office and tells me I can't write—this is a guy who can't write for shit. He reassigns the memo to another associate—Field, I think.''

''Do you think it was a sexual thing?'' Voorhees asked. ''Mallorn always had trouble controlling his eyeballs.''

''His eyeballs were one thing,'' Urquart said. ''His lips, chin, and nose were three square inches of the —I don't know the word to describe it. Boy, now *there* was someone who was physically repulsive. But I don't think that was it. Mallorn knew I thought he was slimy. He used to pad—I mean really pad. He'd bill ten hours on days he did virtually nothing. He knew that I knew he did, too. One time I saw him looking through opposing counsel's briefcase. I learned a lesson.'' Urquart laughed. ''Never leave your briefcase unguarded around a lawyer! I don't know,'' she continued, then paused. Her voice grew more reflective. ''Maybe he had to assert his power. But I really don't think it was that. It was more venal than that. He was a fake, he was a hack. A year away from 'The Big P'—that's how he used to refer to partnership, 'The Big P.' An asshole. A real asshole. So the next time he asks me to do something, I don't do it.''

''You, like, just didn't do it?'' asked Voorhees.

"No," Urquart said, "I would prefer—it's such a perfect word, isn't it?—not to."

Jansen clapped in mock applause.

"It didn't stop them from making him partner," Voorhees said.

"No," Urquart said, "it didn't."

"I hear he's in deep trouble," Voorhees added. "He's making not a whole lot more than a senior associate. I wonder how Elleridge is?"

"Elleridge!" Jansen exclaimed.

"Never did care too much for old Morton, did you?" said Voorhees.

Jansen was shaking his head slowly, a look of anguish on his face. "God—Morton Elleridge. I'll never forget it. The afternoon of the day Alex Gilchrist was passed over for partner. I was in the john, taking a leak, and Gilchrist was taking a leak, too, when who happens to walk in but the Silver Shithead himself, who steps up to the urinal and asks Gilchrist, 'Well, Alec'—he always called Gilchrist Alec, though his name was Alex—'well, Alec, how are things?' Gilchrist looks at him, his eyes all bloodshot—you could tell he'd been crying. This is your kind of guy who'd go three days without sleep for The Big P. Though destined never to be a member of the firm, Gilchrist happens, urinating, to be holding his own member, when Elleridge says to him, 'Not the large things, Alec. How are the small things?' "

Everyone laughed.

The night air had turned breezy and cool, the sky jet-black except for a thin silver light around the moon and a few patches of dark purple clouds. Jansen asked the waitress for the check, which he picked up. We walked along the esplanade away from the harbor, toward South End Avenue, where there were taxis. Jansen was talking to Voorhees about a deal he was working on. Urquart—an associate counsel for a securities firm—was telling me about her two-year-old, the problems she was having with her—"she's Dominican and has three children of her own"—how tired she is when she comes home from work. Her husband, an investment banker, was under a lot of pressure, too.

"Everything," she said, then paused. "The acceleration. Everything's moving so fast! The mind has to be so fast! It takes so much energy just to find time —any time—to just slow it all down a little. I know that sounds a bit dire, but that's not how I mean it. There's a lot, there really is a lot, of money around —no one has any idea how much there is. But things are contracting at the same time, too. Sometimes I image it. All these pools of money floating around out there—wherever 'there' is. All of us trying to attach ourselves to some part of them whatever way—by ourselves, with others—we can. Wylie. Carl Wylie, for example. Wylie is wherever the money is—Singapore, Mexico City, L.A. The only question is who gets it, and how much, and who helps whom get what. I get my one hundred thousand plus, plus bonus, a year, after the government takes half. Wylie—what difference does it make, and to whom, if Wylie makes seven hundred fifty a year or a million two? I have a friend from high school—she's downtown over here, in one of those small offices in an old office building

on Maiden Lane. She does admiralty law. She's with
a small admiralty-law firm. I have no idea what admiralty law is. She tells me, opaquely, it has to do
with things on boats, on ships. She's attaching herself
to a pool of money, too—of a different quality and
quantity, that's all. I saw this thing in the paper—a
regional plan for the next century. Job banks. You go
into a job bank and connect up with a client, anywhere. Where? Tehran?''

"Look!'' Voorhees said, as we came to an inlet
where several luxury yachts were docked. A balustrade separated the inlet from a plaza between it and
the office towers of the World Financial Center, which
loomed massively around us. "Words!''

"Words?'' Jansen asked. "What about that foreign object on top of that enormous yacht over there.
What is *that*?''

"What do you think it is? It's a helicopter,'' Voorhees said. "Your own tiny, personal helicopter on top
of your own huge yacht. Me—I want to know what
this says.''

He stood where the words, in capital letters, be-
gan. "It's some kind of quotation,'' he said, reading
out loud as he walked beside the balustrade. "CITY
OF THE WORLD FOR ALL RACES ARE HERE ALL THE
LANDS OF THE EARTH MAKE CONTRIBUTIONS HERE CITY
OF THE SEA CITY OF . . .''

He stopped. "Over there,'' he said. He nodded his
head toward a man and woman walking across the
plaza. "I know him from somewhere. Where do I
know him from?''

Urquart turned to Jansen. She asked him to finish

reading where Voorhees left off. He looked ahead, where the quotation ended. "Walt Whitman," he said. "CITY OF THE SEA CITY OF TALL FACADES OF MARBLE AND IRON PROUD AND PASSIONATE CITY METTLESOME MAD EXTRAVAGANT CITY WALT WHITMAN."

All Great Problems Come from the Streets

"A REVOLUTION," JUDGE CELIA DAY SAID.

"A revolution?" I asked.

"A revolution."

"But who?"

"Who! Everyone, that's who! The corruption's palpable. Everyone's sitting in front of their television sets watching it. Civility! No one believes there's any anymore! Fragments—yes. But an integral part of the way that we do things? So what do you think happens when no one believes there's any real civility anymore? Politicians! It doesn't matter which side they say they're on—each of them backed by his own small army, and I mean army, too, of lobbyists and lawyers who haven't the slightest care for what is happening in people's lives."

Day straightened her body, staring at me in silence. She was sitting in her burgundy leather chair behind her desk in chambers, on one of the upper floors of the new federal courthouse in lower Manhattan. She leaned over and adjusted the white tulips in a glass vase on her desk, and then sat back again, still silent. It was around four-thirty, an early November afternoon, and we'd just been over a draft of a report for the City Bar Association on political criticism of federal court decisions. Day was tallish and trim, her shoulder-length hair highlighted blond, but what you noticed first were her wide blue and green eyes set behind oval-shaped silver-rimmed glasses. Her conversation fluctuated between rushes of talk and a calm, cool deliberateness, punctuated by long silences. She looked directly at you, intent on making eye contact, and her manner was friendly, even when she was argumentative or contentious. "This time around," she added, "it's crime. Next time, what will it be? Blame the judges for not stopping a war? Drugs? Our fault! Social insanity? Our fault! As if *we* are the ones who make the laws."

Day had been a federal judge for seven years. After graduating from Georgetown Law Center in sixty-nine, she worked several years for the Federal Trade Commission in Washington. She then practiced three years with a large Washington firm before going to work, in the late seventies, in the United States Attorney's office in Manhattan. After successfully prosecuting a number of highly visible drug- and weapons-smuggling cases in the early eighties, she was named a chief assistant. She was appointed to the federal bench by President Bush, with the support of both New York senators, one a Republican, the other a Democrat. "I belong to no political party," she made a point of saying. "Don't get me wrong," she quickly added. "That's not to say that I don't know something about politics." I asked her what she meant by politics and she answered, without hesitation, "Politics is the will to gain and keep power. There's a big difference, though," she said, "a very big difference, between appreciating politics and being a politician." I asked what the difference was. "I don't have to do anything to gain or keep power," she replied. "I am in this job for as long as I want."

"But," I said, "you exert power. Doesn't that make you political?"

"Of course I exert power," Day shot back. "I'm a federal judge. I am a member of the third branch of the government of the United States of America. But I don't actively exert power over people's minds. I do not do that. That's what politicians do. I do not. Law"—she raised her finger for emphasis—"exerts power over people's minds, no question about that. But I am not the law. My responsibility is to interpret and enforce the law. What do I do all day?" She stopped. "Discern. I am constantly discerning. I discern things."

"Doesn't interpreting and discerning involve personal, even political, judgment?" I asked.

"Of course it does," Day said. "So what? You control it, that's all. Our commission is to keep our personal predispositions under control. Sometimes people want you to, other times they don't. It usually has to do with *their* personal predispositions, not mine. Don't forget, either, that it can cut both ways —if you control what you personally feel, then there's

not much room for mercy. Politics! It never even enters your mind! Do you think I'm thinking about a
congressman from eastern Pennsylvania when I'm
trying to put together a jury for a three-month trial?
Robert Jackson had it right—what we do is by force
of our commission. We are *forced* to discern the law
as we see it. We are *forced* to enforce it."

Clasping both hands around the armrests of her
chair, Day slowly lifted herself up. "I have a spinal
problem," she said when she was standing. "I'm
missing vertebrae. One day"—she smiled—"I'll be
crippled. I also don't know how to sit still, which can
be a problem, especially if you're a judge." She began
pacing behind her desk. "Don't mind me," she said.
"It's an old habit of mine. So," she asked, "you want
to know what I think about lawyers?" She stopped,
then started pacing again, a bemused look on her
face.

"I'm at the end of a trial—yesterday there's an
adjournment. So I decide to play hooky and take most
of the morning for myself. I'm getting a late start—I
don't plan on being in chambers until eleven—I'm on
the subway when, at Fifty-ninth Street, a young
woman gets on and sits down across from me, and
what's the first thing I see? Her bra! There is this
girl, in a very expensive black suede jacket—unbut-
toned, hanging to the sides—wearing a totally sheer
white blouse, I mean completely transparent, not like
anything you'd buy in a store, through which you can
see every detail of a very expensive, low-cut—like
something you'd get in Neiman Marcus—white lace
bra! Here I was in one of my contemplative moods
when, suddenly, on the train at Fifty-ninth Street,

sitting down directly across from me, there is this girl in a mini-mini, gold flats, carrying a small gold leather purse, a pinkish-rose lipstick on her kewpie-doll lips, these large brown, gamine—I think that's the right word, gamine—eyes, her small breasts spilling out of a very tight, very expensive white lace bra. Ten-thirty in the morning. I'm thinking to myself, this must be seen to be believed! Shoulder-length blond braids, rhinestone barrettes, and"—Day laughed—"a straw hat. She's wearing a straw hat on the Lexington Avenue subway! Turned up at the brim, an artificial yellow flower attached to the band. She looks like Daisy Mae in the old Li'l Abner comic strip—the old Al Capp comic strip—which, I'm sure, she's never even seen. I'm looking at her, and realizing she can't be much older than my daughter—I have a sixteen-year-old daughter, she's in her junior year at Horace Mann in the Bronx. Daisy Mae is two or three years older than my daughter Susan.

"I'll let you in on a secret," Day said. "*No one* sees me and thinks 'federal judge.' I'll be in a restaurant beside a table of lawyers, all of them loud, talking at the top of their voices—the reason for most mistrials, you know. Lawyers' big mouths. When I'm on the subway, I look like who? I've got my designer sunglasses on, I'm wearing a gray suit, *The Wall Street Journal* in my lap—I look like a banker. I'm looking at this girl—she couldn't care less. She was chewing gum."

Day took a paper clip from her desk and began unraveling it as she continued to pace. "I've got a good friend who's a Family Court judge," she said. "In Brooklyn. She says there are lawyers who come before her on the bench chewing away. *That* I do not see here. I asked her what she does about it. 'What do you think I do?' she says. 'I tell them to take the goddamn gum out of their mouths!' She said she had a lawyer come into her court once—earring, ponytail, T-shirt, jeans, a blue pin-striped suit coat. The T-shirt had AMERICANS written across it. She said she asked him why he wasn't wearing a tie.

"So there I am," Day continued, tossing the paper clip into the wastebasket and then sitting down again, her shoulders back and her body forward on the edge of her chair, "not quite minding my own business, while the guy running the train's got a heavy foot on the pedal—we're moving psychotically fast, rocking back and forth, while I, of course, am imagining a disaster." She tapped her finger against her head. "This is why lawyers are sick. I'm already imagining the lawsuit I'm going to bring against the Metropolitan Transit Authority. I've even decided who my lawyer's going to be—a go-for-the-jugular type with an I-almost-became-a-priest choirboy look on his face, who loves money. Like Terry Gallagher. I'd hire him in a minute. *Worse*, I imagine myself dead, and how much of the wrongful-death action will go into my estate, and, among my heirs, who, in probate, will get what. All this is going through my head while my peripheral vision—on automatic pilot—is picking up every single man on the subway, of every age, staring, I mean staring at this girl, like this"—Day opened her eyes as wide as she could. "They can't take their eyes off her! One character in particular. He's in his late twenties, I'd say, sitting right next to her, right across from me. When this girl gets on the train and sits down beside him he moves his head and looks at her —I mean moves it—like this, laterally, ninety degrees. He then gets up, crosses the aisle, pushes himself in right beside me, and starts staring at her. The instant I see him—I think to myself, lawyer! I'm actually smiling to myself—I do that a lot when I'm on the bench. I'm tempted to turn to him and say something like, 'Hello, I'm Judge Celia Day of the United States District Court for the Southern District of New York. Haven't I seen you before? You're with Crane & Swartout, aren't you?'"

Day put both her palms flat on her desk, slowly pushing her body up again. "How," she asked, standing, "could I tell he was a lawyer? Do you know how many lawyers I've seen in my life? Thousands. Tens of thousands. Well"—she smiled to herself—"after a while you know one when you see one. A doctor I know"—she was pacing again—"a ranter and raver, a scientist at heart. His latest thing—phenotypes. Do you know what a phenotype is?" I said that I didn't. "A phenotype is how an organism appears. The observable characteristics of an organism as they appear as a result of the interaction between the organism's genetic structure and its environment."

Day stopped, with a look on her face as if she'd suddenly remembered something. She went over to her desk and took a fountain pen—a Montblanc—from a drawer. She carefully unscrewed the cap and then took a piece of stationery from another drawer, on which she wrote, in large script, while standing, a half page of words.

"There," she said, putting the cap back on, leaving the pen on top of the piece of paper. "Anyway," she said, "a phenotype is what you get when the genotype—a genotype is the genetic constitution of an organism—interacts with its environment. It's really the expression of what the genotype is—the characteristics of the genotype in a certain place, at a certain time. My doctor friend is the theoretical type—he makes all of this into a theory. One phenotype—one expression of the human genotype—is what he calls the 'nineteen-nineties American urban drug addict.' Heroin, crack, methamphetamine, nicotine, alcohol addiction, more or less at one time or other, *plus* AIDS, hepatitis, diabetes. Caffeine, too, I'm sure," Day said, then laughed. "I saw a beggar the other day in front of the new Federal Building on Broadway—in one hand, a Starbuck's paper coffee cup for you to put money in, in the other, a Starbuck's cup filled with, probably, something like a double mocha with a touch of cinnamon. Another of the doctor's phenotypes?" Day asked. "The doctor phenotype. Observable characteristics? First on the list, an absolute terror of death. Then, an absolute terror of contracting a viral disease, and—this I like—a propensity toward patriarchy. Then there's his lawyer phenotype. Characteristic number one? Liars. Liars! He says he had an uncle from Scotland who used to pronounce lawyer 'lie-arr-err,' and then scratch himself like a baboon. He imitates his uncle—'lie-arr-err, lie-arr-err.' I really don't know how he expected me to respond. What was I supposed to say? 'Oh, that's nice'?"

Day stopped and pressed her hands against her lower back. "The nice lawyer fellow on the subway? The phenotype. Hair slicked back just a bit—

moussed. Conservatively moussed hair. He was carrying a five- or six-hundred-dollar trench coat. Wearing a beautiful soft navy-blue Italian designer suit, a silk print tie . . .''

"No suspenders?" I asked.

Day arched her eyebrows. "No," she said, with mock weariness. "No. Though the phenotype could be wearing suspenders. Red, I'd say. Red-patterned. Or dark blue with a maroon stripe. His shoes were wing-tips—five hundred dollars, easy. He had a soft black leather briefcase, which he put between us on the subway seat—the kind you really can't put very much into. There was a similar type—a different phenotype, but a similar type—when I was that age. Harold Rock—honest to God, that was his name, Harold Rock. Well, this young man—phenotype was written all over him! Relaxed and assured, yet at the same time that look of lust and abandon—it's hard to describe—but you know what I mean. I looked at him through the corner of my left eye—he was looking straight at the girl with enormous confidence. You know, that look—and letting you know it—of knowing something you don't. Of being above, somehow—it's not quite power. I don't know what it is—it's more than confidence. Then there's the girl! What's *her* phenotype? There's clearly a thing going on between them—he knows that she knows that he has every intention of getting what he wants—after, of course, they decide what it is he wants. All this is happening in a four- to five-minute time span. We stop at Grand Central, then Union Square. The subway doors open, Daisy Mae gets up, Crane & Swartout follows—ten forty-five in the morning! I can see our dashing young officer of the court calling his secretary to say he won't be in until after lunch—that he's been 'detained.' Me? My little morning show is over. I get to chambers and there are twenty phone calls on my desk and one of my law clerks in a panic—which she ought to be—because she's missed a deadline I told her was absolutely absolute—which it was."

Day glanced at her watch, then asked if I'd like something to drink. I said no. She picked up her phone and asked whoever answered it for a glass of ginger ale, which her secretary then brought in to her with a glass of ice. She sat down again slowly, careful of her back. She poured some ginger ale into the glass and left it there on her desk.

"My problem is," she said, "I get into things too much. I talk too much, too, which"—she shrugged—"used to bother me, but doesn't anymore. I know how to listen, too—I'm an extremely attentive listener. People who say 'I'm not a talker, I'm a listener,' it's nonsense. If you know how to talk, you know how to listen. If you know how to talk, you're listening to what you're saying. It's those who don't listen to what they're saying who are the most insufferable people on earth—it doesn't matter if they talk a lot or not. My problem isn't how much I talk—my problem is that the older I get, the more I find myself over this line in my head, where I'm just watching. Perhaps the finest lawyer I've ever known used to say—it was one of his cardinal rules—if you look hard enough for an answer, you'll find it. Everything's there, you just have to look for it. That's how my memory works. Events, entire pieces of testimony—I *see* them. As if they're part of a picture. Have you ever seen *One-Eyed Jacks*? Marlon Brando, Karl Malden, Katy Jurado? It's one of my favorite movies. Nineteen sixty-one. There's a scene where Brando's face, in full color, fills the entire screen, while he moves a toothpick from one side of his mouth to the other. That's the sort of thing that's really interesting in a courtroom. The things that go on in a courtroom! Someone once asked me what the strangest thing I'd ever seen in my courtroom was. Well, I've seen a lot of strange scenes, but do you know what came to mind? A government witness on the witness stand snorting cocaine. Matted hair, bloodshot eyes, specks of something or other on his shirt, he's sitting five feet away from me making this snorting sound into his handkerchief. He'd put the coke in his handkerchief. There he was, inhaling away. I have a nervous habit—I scratch my cuticles. If I get bored, I don't even know I'm doing it. I look over and there's a juror staring at me. What goes on in people's minds in a courtroom—*that* you don't see in the movies or on TV! The people who aren't talking are looking—and when you're looking you're either listening or your mind is wandering—God, how the mind wanders! I've never fallen asleep on the bench, though I have colleagues who have. Their heads fall back, their mouths open, they start falling out of their chairs. I can remember . . ."

Day stopped and smiled. "I'd better not," she said. "There's a story I could tell, but my better judgment tells me I'd better not." She then stood up again. "I'm sorry about all this getting up and down," she went on, "but it really hasn't been a very good day for my back." She rotated her neck several times, then shook both her hands. "So," she said, "what do you think? What my doctor friend said about lawyers. I don't think it can be disputed, do you?"

"I'm not really sure I want to answer that," I said.

"Do you think it really can't be disputed?" asked Day. "It's inherent in the process." The tone of her voice was matter-of-fact. "Those who aren't part of it—who don't do it—are incapable of understanding it. Lawyers know too much. If you know too much, how don't you lie? Everything you say has another meaning. The posturing, the playacting, arguing over the smallest things, the narcissism, the beyond-belief egomania—it's all part of that. Too much meaning. I once had a rather unpleasant argument with quite an eminent philosopher—a political philosopher, to be precise—a chaired professor at Columbia. I got really carried away—I have a bad habit of jabbing my finger when I argue and he told me to stop. You know when you get carried away and you get embarrassed? But I was angry. I don't get angry often, but once I am, I get very angry. This guy's written several books on political theory, one of them won—I think it was —a National Book Award. I don't remember. He was the one who was confrontational. The legal system— his voice was extremely loud—is corrupt. It has nothing to do with truth! So I ask him—I was trying to keep my voice as composed as I could—what is truth. He laughs at me. He stands right there and laughs at me! 'Who are you,' he says, 'Pontius Pilate?' Pontius Pilate! Like I'm his graduate student!"

Day paused. When she continued, her voice was slower, more even. "The patronizing son of a bitch," she said. "I remember reading an article somewhere about how spooky—that was the word used—how spooky lawyers are. Lawyers are spooky because they have no idea what real people—those were the words used, real people—think about them. Lawyers have no idea what real people think of them—when, for example, on TV, they, the lawyers, while the whole world is watching them, there, on TV, they manipulate the truth. On TV! God forbid that a real lawyer, on or off TV, doesn't really care if 'real people' think he's spooky or not. That a real lawyer has an ethical obligation—I repeat, an ethical obligation—to defend his or her client, and when you're a public servant, which I have been most of my career, your client is the people. You have an obligation under oath to defend your client within the boundaries of the law. I love it! You're not a real person if you're a lawyer! Real people know what real truth is! I asked this jerk how he would set up a truth-finding process in a court of law. You should have seen the look on his face. Everything shifted. I used as an example an antitrust case—I walked him through the statute and presented him with the issues. Suddenly I'm someone with an idea—some idea—of the real world, aware of things this clown's never even imagined. It's such a strange business. On the one hand, you're treated like someone special. On the other, like you're an idiot."

Day looked at her watch again. I said that I should be going. She said to wait, that she had something to tell one of her clerks, and left for a few minutes. "No, I think this is worth talking about," she said when she returned. "The lying." She sat down. "The deception. It's not easy to talk about, nor is it easy to explain. Remember, lawyers are the ones who invented spin. Spin's a public-relations term for what every lawyer knows how to do—if you have to, you change the story. How low is spin among the circles of deceit? I'd say lower than keeping your own counsel—when what you're really doing is not providing information to a person who trusts you to do so. How about, 'I didn't do that,' when, in fact, you did? In my judicious opinion? A very low form of deceit. It's one thing to say, 'That's not what I said'—which is going on a lot these days, everyone covering, pardon my language, their proverbial asses. But it's an altogether different thing to say that a document never existed when, in fact, it did, and you, or your client, destroyed it. That I don't recommend. Double-talk, triple-talk, saying you're going to do something when you know you're not going to"—Day shrugged—"what can you do? But saying that something happened when it didn't? Saying that something didn't happen when it did? This is a business in which everyone relies on representations. This is a business in which no one ever forgets, no one ever forgives—a business in which no one *ought* ever to forget or forgive anyone who goes beyond those extremely tolerable thresholds of deceit into one of those morally . . ." Day stopped. "Let's just use the word 'wrong.' When you do something no one would argue is wrong. My experience is, when you do something no one would argue is wrong, you don't want another lawyer having that on you because—here, if you ask me, is the mind-set—a lawyer will get even. It's how the system—is there a verb *retribute*? That's how the system retributes itself. It really does. How do they say it on the street?—'what you do comes back on you.' It may take a while, but you make a material misrepresentation of fact to another lawyer, you'd better be prepared to be hit, and I mean hit, and hit hard. The equivalent of being, at the very least, blindsided with a crowbar.

"I probably shouldn't be telling you this," Day said. "A lawyer I worked with when I practiced in D.C.—he's a managing partner now, the same firm. He lost—his client lost—real money because of a remarkably foul lie by the lawyer on the other side, who, at the time, was very powerful, a big shot, around fifty. My friend was thirty. This was twenty years ago. My friend waits. The other lawyer is in intensive care dying of stomach cancer—he's served with papers. 'Of course,' my friend says—he's very quiet, mild-mannered—'it's a perfectly valid lawsuit,' and"—Day smiled—"'I'm sure it is. In fact, my friend's firm isn't bringing it. Another firm is. There are tubes in this now old man's nostrils. He can't move, but he still can see, and he still can read—he's being sued individually for five million dollars. Paul —my friend—says, 'What a shame—just think, he's going to have to go out now and hire a lawyer.' Paul said he heard that when the other lawyer saw the complaint—remember, he was in intensive care—he started pulling the tubes out of his nostrils. I think Paul was joking about that," Day said. "You never know about Paul. He sounds so sincere—the way he looks and talks—and he is, but sometimes you don't know when he's kidding you."

Day took her glasses off. "I probably shouldn't be telling you this, either. I'm sure that you know who he is. A very prominent retired circuit judge. Quite distinguished. Extraordinarily savvy. Most of my colleagues—though they'll deny it—don't like him. Actually, they hate his guts. I'm not sure I like him, either—but, finally, I respect him, which, these days, is saying a lot. He was a friend of Lyndon Johnson—knew him well, in fact, and had real misgivings about him, but he always repeats two Lyndon Johnson stories. One was Johnson's remark about then House Minority Leader and—let me add—political point man for the movement to impeach William Douglas, Gerald Ford—I should say President Ford. That Ford couldn't walk and chew gum at the same time. The impeach-Douglas thing was, by the way—pardon the parenthesis—later. The Republicans loathed Douglas the way the Democrats loathe Clarence Thomas now. Douglas was letting everyone in Washington know that he thought Nixon—whom he'd despised since World War II when Nixon was a lawyer for the Office of Price Administration, before his House Committee on Un-American Activities days—was a fascist. He'd use the word, too. End of parenthesis.

"Well"—Day took a piece of tissue from her desk drawer and began cleaning her glasses—"this Second Circuit judge used to say that a good lawyer must be able to walk and chew gum at the same time. He'd then add that Gerry Ford was a graduate of his alma mater, the Yale Law School, and, from what he knew, never chewed gum. He also reminded you that Ford's Attorney General, Edward Levi, was one of the most respected lawyers in the country at the time, and that Ford appointed John Paul Stevens, another superb lawyer, to the Supreme Court. The other Johnson story—Lyndon Johnson! Now *there*"—Day folded her glasses and put them in a case, holding it as she spoke—"was someone who wasn't a lawyer with the ultimate lawyer's mind. Johnson told one of his minions to spread the rumor around Washington that one of his enemies slept—literally—with hogs. When the young politico—a Bobby Kennedy protégé type who'd never even seen a real hog in his life—told the President that the story just wasn't true, Johnson looked at him through those slitty eyes of his and said, 'I know it ain't true. I just want to watch the prick deny it.'

"We should start getting out of here," Day suddenly said. She stood up and walked over to her credenza, and began rummaging through a pile of papers and books. "Take a look from here before you leave," she said, motioning me over to the windows, while she paged through a document. "The buildings in Chinatown"—she looked up—"are mostly from the end of the last century and the beginning of this one. It looks like a small town from up here, doesn't it? Those clouds over the East River—sometimes the sky will turn dark green, dark gray, black, all within a minute or two. You can actually watch a storm—snowstorms, too—blow in off the ocean.

"We can keep talking while I'm getting my things together," she went on. "I'll tell you what I think the question ought to be," she said. "Why. The question ought to be why. *Why* the law is what it is."

I said I wasn't sure what she meant. "No one ever

asks why," she said. "Why is the law what it is. That lawyer I mentioned earlier to you—the one who said that if you look hard enough you'll find what you're looking for. He also used to say *don't* count on the courts. That real power exists outside the courts. Put pressure on a court, all the pressure that you can, and if you win, fine, take it, and if you lose, fight it —do whatever you can to achieve your objective, but don't ever count on a court. Real power doesn't exist in the courts. He was so right. You have discretion in this job, but you'd be surprised how little. It's taken me an embarrassingly long time to realize that there's a big difference between having a bit of discretion and having real power. It is a very important distinction. A very, very, very important distinction.

"There!" Day snapped her briefcase shut. "All set. Let's get out of here."

On our way out, she stopped to speak with both her clerks. "One is shy," she said as we walked to the elevators. "The other's not. You have to teach them to say what they think. Some get it right away. Others, it takes time. Then there are those who never get it."

Outside, she asked if I'd walk her to the subway. We walked on Pearl Street beside the old federal courthouse—the New York State Supreme Court building was across the street—toward Foley Square.

"I'll tell you, too, who I think a lot about," Day said. "Children. I know"—she quickly added— "everyone does. But that's not how I mean it. I see so many kinds of people in my line of work, all sorts of different people. The one thing I can tell you for certain is there are a lot of people living in the ex-

treme. Under circumstances that astound me. All that
I'm saying is, children see. Don't think for a second
they don't. We did. They do, too. Is anyone thinking
about what the children are seeing? You've got these
kids—kids in their late teens, early twenties—they're
in my court for God knows what. Counterfeiting. I
had a case—kids passing counterfeit twenty-dollar
bills downtown here, around Wall Street. They've got
this air of banality about them—and know what? It
stinks. It really stinks. You try to figure out what
they're thinking. You can't. It's impossible. You
know you're going to put them in prison, and they
know you know it, and they try to look right through
you, they stare at you, you've got no idea what's going
on in their minds—they're sullen. No, that's not the
right word. Insolent. That's the word I want. Insolent. Toward you, toward themselves, toward life itself. Even their peers on Wall Street—the young
financiers, the ones right out of school, the younger
ones—they think they're the first ones ever to be financiers. Insolent. Do you know what else? Scared.
That's what I think. A lot of it going around these
days—insolent and scared.''

We walked to the subway entrance under the arch
of the Manhattan Municipal Building. It was getting
dark. The air had turned damp and cold. It had begun to rain.

''Let's go over here and talk,'' Day said. We stood
beside a large pillar, away from the flow of people on
their way to the subway. Day looked directly at me.
''Another thing,'' she said, ''is liberty. Americans
love their liberty. Every one of us with our own sense
of liberty. Everyone with a different sense of when

the law should protect our liberty. Always—though this, no one thinks about—at the expense of someone else's. No one in complete agreement with anyone else about any of it, either. Part of this country's fundamental law is a Bill—it's a *Bill*—of Rights. The first time in the history of the world a government provided its citizens with the right to use government—through its courts—to protect their rights *against* the government! You wonder why we've had our problems! Know what else? People will fight for liberty. They'll kill for it. Think of how much of human history is people killing in the name of liberty. People will fight in the streets over liberty. I don't remember who said it—that all great problems come from the streets. Do you know what the definition of justice is on the street? You get what you deserve, that's what it is. You get what you deserve. Now, isn't that interesting?''

Day folded her arms around her trench coat. ''It's gotten cold,'' she said, shaking her shoulders. She looked at me again, almost staring. ''What if,'' she said, ''just what if the law we have is the law we deserve?''

She broke into a smile. ''You're looking at me as if I'm out of my mind! I'm serious! It's a rather democratic concept, actually. I can see it on talk TV. 'Is the law we have the law we deserve?' How does it go?—from the Pledge of Allegiance? 'One nation, under God, indivisible . . .' But what if''—Day's voice changed tone—''it isn't indivisible? What if, in fact, it's very divisible—divided, dividing, all over the place? What if, instead, it's one nation of private militias, one of police, one of women, one of men, an-

other of whatever race you are, still another one of
your religion, one nation of armed forces, another
of employers, one of employees, another of those
who drug themselves, one nation of unemployed, of
those who have had abortions, another of those who
haven't, and then, of course, all those nations com-
prised of those either of upwardly mobile or mobilely
downward economic status. What, then, would be the
law that we deserve? You tell me.

"A former clerk of mine—he works down here. At
the same firm, perhaps, as our subway lothario. Six
months into his clerkship he says—he's quite agitated
about it—that there no longer is a nation. What is
really going on is that we're in a state of civil wars.
A young lawyer who thinks about the society he lives
in—a Generation X lawyer has thoughts like this?
Well, I can tell you, just because they may be insolent, and they are scared, doesn't mean that there
aren't some very serious sorts in their twenties roam-
ing around out there. So I asked him—nice image,
isn't it, a state of civil wars?—if what he says is true,
then what happens, I asked him, to the law, to lawyers? What kind of law, what kind of lawyers, do you
have when your civil order is, in fact, in a state of
civil wars? What, for example, would have happened
if the truck that exploded under the World Trade
Center had been about two hundred feet away from
where it was, and an entire tower—all one hundred
ten floors—collapsed? How many legal relationships
—civil, criminal, federal, state, municipal, international—would have been affected? Tell me—who
among those affected would have gotten what he de-
served? Who would have gotten it for him? All great

problems come from the streets? What happens when one of them—one small fraction of just one of them —enters the office of the United States Department of Justice? It can happen, you know. One day an Assistant United States Attorney receives a package in the mail. In it there's a briefcase—just like this one I've got. Inside it, a sawed-off shotgun rigged to a device.''

Day propped her briefcase on her knee and snapped it open. Her eyes widened. "Like this!" she said. "In the stomach! Do you know what happens if you're shot in the gut, a foot away, by a sawed-off shotgun? What if the briefcase is just a bit slanted— like this?'' She turned her briefcase toward me. "*Whoosh!* There's not going to be much of your government attorney's head left, now, is there? It's what happened to Judge Lowenstein. The same way. Fortunately, in our case, an F.B.I. agent was with this assistant at the time. He told her that he'd better open it, that you never know. He opens it from the side— *pow*! A huge hole in the office wall.''

Day closed her briefcase. "Tomorrow, first thing," she said, then paused to catch her breath. "A sentencing. Can I run it past you? Is that all right? Then I've got to be going. I know I'm keeping you." She shook her shoulders. "I should have worn my winter coat," she said. "Look. I appreciate it. I'll be fast. The facts." She took another breath. "A forty-year-old woman. She's—well—let's just say she's a citizen. She pays a lot of money to have her husband killed, but it doesn't come off. She's arrested and pleads guilty to conspiracy to murder. Under the sentencing guidelines I've no choice—nine years, no parole. I can reduce her sentence if there are mitigating circumstances. But I have to have really good reasons."

Suddenly a gust of wind blew rain near where we were standing. We moved farther under the Municipal Building arch, beside another pillar. Day continued. "Her lawyers have a psychiatric report done," she said. "First-rate. One of the best psychiatrists in the country. University of Chicago. Excellent. It so happens that this woman's marriage was arranged. It so happens, too, that every time this woman has sex with her husband, it's forced on her. The violence is graphic—you could even say perverse. Ugly stuff— sodomy, rape. This is on the record—the woman's never had an orgasm, which her husband attributes to her having affairs. So what does he do? More violence, under the guise of sex."

"Battered woman's syndrome," I said.

"Maybe that's what it is. I don't know. I've got to sentence her. This woman's pled guilty to conspiracy to commit murder. She's going to go to prison. I have to decide how much of the next—at a minimum—nine years she's going to live in a federal penitentiary. But that's not all. There's more. Every single time the woman's been in court her husband's been with her. They sit beside each other. They talk. You'd think they were just like any other husband and wife. Oh, I almost forgot. The husband has never denied his wife's allegations."

"He's never denied her allegations?"

"Never. That's not all, either. Husband and wife are in business together. A very lucrative three-, four-million-dollar-a-year import business. There's a five-million-dollar life-insurance policy on the husband's life. Since the wife's been in jail, the business has been falling apart. She's the brains of the operation. Without her, the husband doesn't know how to run things. Finally—children. A boy and a girl. A ten- and an eight-year-old. Beautiful children. There are pictures of both of them. They're part of the record."

Day stopped. She started walking toward the subway. "Let me know," she said over her shoulder, "when you're ready to go over the next draft of the report."

Transactional

THE DEEPEST, DARKEST SECRET. I LIKE THAT. I want to get back to that. But first," Thomas Rao said, "Karpinski. How is that you know Richard, again?

"Through a mutual friend," I said. "Charlie Serra."

"I know Charlie Serra. He's a real estate partner—Canfield Stutz Yeager & Linsares, isn't he? I met him at something or other Richard put together. Respectable enough guy, if I remember right."

Rao got up from his desk and walked over to a small kitchen area and made himself a cup of tea. "How well do you know Karpinski?" he asked, returning to his desk and sitting down. I said I didn't know him at all, that Charlie Serra told me that he would be an interesting person to talk to. "But," I said, "when I called Karpinski, he suggested that I call you."

Rao laughed. "Richard is very careful about who he talks to. I've known Karpinski since the third grade, you know—we grew up together. Yonkers. Karpinski was a lunatic. He and his two brothers—they were even more insane than he was. Street-smart, though, the Karpinskis—all of them. Richard is no one's fool."

Rao blew on his tea to cool it, then took a sip from the large pewter cup he held with both hands. His office was in the old Standard Oil building, which looks out over the small wedge of Bowling Green where Broadway begins in front of the old United States Custom House, a city-block granite Beaux Arts building which now houses a United States Bank-ruptcy Court and the National Museum of the American Indian. A quarter to nine in the morning, the January air, outside, was icy cold, the sky a bright crystal blue. Beyond the Custom House, Battery Park was flooded with light, New York Harbor a shimmering aquamarine. "I like getting to work early," Rao said, placing his cup on his desk. He stood up and took off his charcoal pin-striped suit jacket. "No later than seven o'clock," he continued, walking over to a closet to hang up his jacket. He then sat down again in a large black leather chair, behind a wide mahogany desk, piles of papers stacked neatly on it. Soft-spoken, his full black hair parted on the side. His manner was intense, yet genial. Unbuttoning the top button of his dark blue shirt, he loosened his yellow print tie. "I'm up at five-thirty every morning," he said. "I am incapable of sleeping past five-thirty. I can get a whole day's work done between the time I get here and when the phone starts ringing.''

Rao propped his elbows on the arms of his chair and folded his hands in front of his chest. ''So,'' he said. ''Karpinski told you to call me. Richard! What a piece of work! I hardly ever see him anymore. We talk on the phone, every other week, maybe. The last time, he launched''—Rao started shaking his head—''into his 'I hate them' litany. 'I hate them all, I hate them all, I hate them all, I hate them all, I hate them all!' 'Who, Richard, do you hate?' 'Them all,' he says. 'Every fucking one of them.' Richard likes talking in absolutes. He hates them all. He means it, too. Every one of them.''

''Who's the 'them'?'' I asked.

''Me and you, that's who. Members of our esteemed profession. This time, in particular, Westin Marshall. Marshall's a lawyer-turned-something-else —in Wessie's case, a venture capitalist. What he is, is, he's inherited millions of dollars and invests it. He was an associate at Caldwell, but was passed over, back in the days they'd float you the whole eight years. Richard's known him for quite a while. I have no idea what kind of business they do with each other, and—to tell you the truth—I really don't want to know. 'A man of means' is how Richard refers to him—Marshall is 'a man of means.' ''

''What does Karpinski do?'' I asked.

''I'm getting to that,'' said Rao. ''It's not that easy a question to answer. Richard . . .'' He was smiling. ''Richard has this routine with Marshall. He asks him how business is, and Marshall always answers the same way, that he's having fun. This has been going on for God knows how long. Marshall has no idea Richard's playing a game with him. 'Fun,' Richard says, 'fun! Fun for Wessie means he's making piles of cash from his piles of cash. Fun for that cocksucker means laundering money through one of his clients and not getting caught.' Cocksucker's a word Richard likes to use a lot. It's embarrassing. He has to be the last heterosexual in the world who uses the word in mixed company. I've told him that—he laughs and says he's always careful to use the word accurately. Another thing, when he's talking he always adds 'she' to 'he.' He'll announce—it doesn't matter what the occasion is—that he's a feminist. One of his raps— he'll say a word like cocksucker, expecting you to wince, which you do. He asks what the problem is. 'You know,' he says in this entirely put-on tone of voice, 'this whole damn country has a genitalia hang-up. Genitalia and melancholia. Am I the only one to have noticed that everyone is hung up on genitalia and everyone is feeling melancholia?' Classic Karpinski. Richard says that if a lawyer says he or she is having fun, what he or she really means is, he or she is making a lot of dough, or, according to Karpinski, he or she is getting some he-or-she action on the side. 'Aren't you going to ask me what kind of action on the side he or she is getting?' he asks me, straight-faced. I tell him I don't want to know what kind of action on the side. It's beyond my imagination, what kind of action Karpinski is getting on the side. I've never been able to figure out what his practice is.''

I said Serra told me that he and Karpinski worked on the purchase of an office building in the West Fifties. Serra was representing an Argentine bank.

"That's what Richard will tell you, that he does real estate. Real estate! Right! It's like my grandfather used to say when he was asked what business he was in—he'd say tomatoes." Rao stopped. "Please," he said, leaning over and taking a quick sip of tea, then sitting back in his chair. "I certainly don't want to give the wrong impression. I in no way wish to impugn Karpinski's integrity. Richard is a solid citizen. A very hard-working—well, actually no one's ever been sure about that. It's another rap of his. 'Have you ever met a lawyer who isn't telling you how hard he works? Working on their hard-ons, that's what they're working on. The women, too—working on imagining them.' He's always saying he's working hard at not having to work hard. He went to law school at night, you know. In Philadelphia. Temple. He worked full-time during the day for a real estate company. He never really told me what he did—I'd get bits and pieces. While he was in law school he told me he'd figured it out. That most people need a lawyer for three things—a will, buying a house, and for a divorce. So what's he do when he gets out of law school? He pretty much goes out on his own—he and this pal of his who speaks fluent Spanish—hustling wills, closings, divorces. They set up shop in Queens near the courthouse. I was at Bolo's the other night and ran into a guy I went to law school with—I went to N.Y.U. He asked me what I was doing. Medical malpractice, I told him. He looked at me as if I was the waiter. What popped into his corporate head was Court Street, the lawyers he sees every morning when he gets on the IRT in Brooklyn Heights to come into the city. The guys who advertise in the subway.

"Well, that's pretty much what Karpinski did," Rao went on, "but Queens-style. He'd wear imported Italian double-breasted linen suits and—I'm not joking—alligator shoes. He'd point at them—'Nice, heh?'—and say they weren't really alligator, that they were dolphin. He did some personal injury, too —I'd send him small, over-threshold auto stuff, and he'd send me stuff he couldn't handle, for which, I should add, he received ample referral fees. He did some immigration, too—though mostly, again, referrals. His divorce practice led to his own—but I won't get into that! He did very well for himself. He's a very good lawyer. He did our will, the work on the condo we bought. High quality. His response when another lawyer looks at him like he's a form of low-life? 'Like I give a flying fuck.' 'Flying fuck.' Another Karpinski favorite."

Rao swung his chair around and stood up. "His most recent foray?" he asked, walking over to the closet where he'd hung his suit jacket. "Entertainment law. Entertainment law!" He took a Chap Stick from his jacket pocket, rubbed his lips with it, then put it back into his coat pocket. "Richard represents *artistes*," he continued, still standing. "Of course, it has nothing to do with the fact that he's been seeing a twenty-five-year-old Puerto Rican actress—who, I must say, is really quite talented, in addition to being gorgeous. She's appeared in a couple of soaps. Richard's office is in SoHo, or NoHo—over on Lafayette, near the East Village. The last time we talked he said he's thinking about moving down here. He sees it as the new downtown cyber-scene. He wants to get onto the Web. *Artistes* on the Web! He's probably going to try hit your buddy Serra's Argentinean bank for a bit of financing. He also said he's thinking about growing a ponytail. He told me he was recently downtown in state supreme court—a real estate bankruptcy case. The trustee—now *there's* a racket!—called him an animal right in front of the judge. He's defending—it has something to do with a bankrupt office building where people are living. Richard's the tenants' lawyer. He told me that he asked that it be put on the record—that, indeed, he was an animal, a gorilla, in fact. I asked him how the other lawyer responded. Karpinski"—Rao laughed—"said that he objected."

The phone rang as Rao was finishing his sentence. He let it ring a couple of times, then walked over to his desk and picked it up. "Yes, yes," he said every few seconds, his eyes still fixed on me. "Fine. See you at ten." He hung up. He stood half staring out the window. "The deepest, darkest secret," he finally said, looking directly at me again, "is the deepest, darkest secret. But before we get into deepest, darkest secrets, let me, first, finish with Karpinski. Karpinski's old man was a milkman. He was a displaced Pole who came here after the war and drove an old beat-up milk truck through lower-middle-class Italian neighborhoods, ours included, delivering milk. I liked Mr. Karpinski—he was always decent to me. When Richard had his practice in Queens—he was leasing a Cadillac at the time—I was at his younger brother's wedding and overheard Mr. Karpinski telling a new in-law that Richard was 'big,' which I never told Richard because I didn't want to hear his reply. Mr. Karpinski loved opera. He was a milkman who loved opera. Richard knows opera well—he knows as much about it as a scholar. He has an incredible opera collection. There's one aria he listens to every morning —he's been doing it for years. He's a runner—he's done marathons. He runs up to ten miles a day. He gets up, runs, and, while he's running, he's listening over and over—he has the most expensive Sony Walkman you can buy—over and over to an absolutely soaringly beautiful bass-and-tenor duet by Bizet from *The Pearl Fishers*, *Au fond du temple saint*, it's called. One final thing about Karpinski," Rao said. "He drinks. Single malt. He buys these eighty-dollar bottles of Mortlach—fifteen-year-old Mortlach —at a place on Madison in the forties. He's one of those drinkers who manage somehow to maintain a sense of what he's doing. Mind over matter, or, in Karpinski's case"—Rao smiled—"'matter over mind. There are lawyers who can drink like that, and they are formidable, too—as long as their livers hold out. The alcohol depresses everyone else, but pumps them right up. Makes them hyperphysical. They can really cut you up."

Rao sat back down, looking thoughtful. "The deepest, darkest secret," he said, then paused. "You can say what you want about lawyers, but one thing —lawyers know how to keep a secret. They really do. Like that Broderick & Williams partner—one of their head honchos, on the board of God knows every bank—murdered up in the Bronx by a male prostitute at one of those fifteen-dollar-an-hour motels off the Cross Bronx. Everyone who knew him said they never suspected a thing. I'm sure it's true, too. This man's not going to be good at keeping a secret? How many secrets about his clients—his banks—went with him to the grave? I'll bet, too, that a couple of his partners—in the midst of their tears—sighed a secret sigh of relief. Please don't misunderstand me—I'm not judging the man. He clearly had his troubles. I'd bet, in fact, there was a secret or two deeper than the Bronx motel. Every lawyer has one or two—or, among the more precocious, three or four—real beauties. Like Karpinski. On a deep dark secret scale of ten, I'd say Karpinski is, clearly, in the eight or nine range."

The phone was ringing again. "Excuse me," Rao said. "I've got to take this." He leaned forward, grabbed the phone, and listened intently for a minute or so. He then said that he was with someone and would have to call back. "I'll call you at five. No, no, I agree," he added. "We have to do something about it. It's a waste of everyone's time. I'm willing. Five."

He hung up. He seemed annoyed. "I'm going to put you in touch with Fred Singleton," he said. "He works the other side. He's very skilled—a bit too intense for me, but, as much as one can expect, moral. At least he keeps his word. He'll be able to fill you in on what I don't."

"You do mostly medical malpractice?"

"Yes. Almost entirely now."

"You must know doctors."

"I know a lot of doctors. We have a doctor associated with our firm. We paid his way through law school. My closest friend is a doctor, a urologist. One of my greatest fears is prostate cancer—my father died of it. Every man will die, if of no other cause, then of prostate cancer—did you know that? I'm also high-risk heart attack or stroke. There's serious heart disease on both sides of my family. They make mistakes, you know, doctors. They also watch each other make mistakes. There are doctors who overdiagnose, like lawyers who overbill—they create work for themselves. I have a lot in common with doctors. Pain, for example. Doctors try to take it away. I try to get compensation for it. I'm in the business of pain—bodily pain. The dichotomy in this culture between bodily injury and mental pain—anyone who knows anything about it knows it's ridiculous. The brain's a very important part of the body. Garrison used to repeat it over and over again—my mentor in this business, Gene Garrison. The brain is a very important part of the body. 'No, of course not,' " Rao went on, in a mock rhetorical voice, " 'the condition of your uterus or your bladder has nothing to do with how you feel, does it?' " He asked if I knew what the heart was. "Do you know what a heart doctor I know says?" he asked, before I could say anything. "The heart is the most important muscle in the body. The heart is *the* most important muscle in the body."

"Have you always done personal injury?"

"Yes."

"How long?"

"Let's see. I'm thirty-seven—I graduated from law school when I was twenty-five—twelve years. This is my thirteenth year. There were, you know, classmates of mine who made twice what I did out of law school. Twice. I went to work for a small plaintiffs' firm and was laughed at. I learned from the best, though. Gene Garrison. The absolute best. Garrison's how old now?—in his sixties. *Harvard Law Review.*

In the same class as—a couple of years behind, maybe—Ralph Nader, whom he knows well. Gene got into products right when it was taking off—like those securities-fraud plaintiffs' lawyers who jumped on the federal class-action rules right when they went into effect. The defense bar wasn't ready for him. Gene's a—I was going to say Buddhist, but he'd disagree with that. What he is, is a student of the body and soul. I mean student. When we first met, after I told him I'd gone to Catholic schools, what's he do? He walks me over to a little religious bookstore behind Trinity Church and buys me Thomas Merton's *Asian Journal*—you know, the Trappist monk?''

Rao looked sideways for a moment, before fixing me with a stare. He'd moved his chair closer to his desk, and put his fingers together in the form of a steeple. "You know"—his voice was lower—"I don't think that much about what I do. Never have. For me, it's always been a long-haul game. Even if you hit the jackpot—which is every lawyer's dream—and I have hit it several times—it's still a long, hard game. The thing that makes me sick to my stomach is the other lawyers . . . Garrison always said that you have to assess the lawyers you're dealing with. He had these exercises. He'd look, for example, at the way a lawyer walked. It's something he learned from actors. You figure out the way a person walks, and you can figure out the way he thinks, the way that he talks, his expressions. Have you ever watched the way lawyers walk? My favorites are the guys who pump their heads up and down, while they're swinging the arm that's not carrying their briefcase—long, arched steps, all juiced-up. He'd also describe souls. It was wild! 'So-and-so's soul looks like . . .' Not only with lawyers, but jurors, judges, too. Clients? The best advice I ever heard. 'You take their pain personally,' Garrison always said, 'and everything else will take care of itself.' That's all you need to know, you know. That's what the best do. That's all they really do.''

The phone was ringing again. Rao answered, saying little. As he listened, he moved the receiver away from his ear, closing, then opening, his eyes. ''No,'' he said softly. ''No! No!'' He raised his voice, almost shouting. He lowered it then to a whisper. ''No. I want to see the X-rays myself. I know more than Thompson knows, anyway. Send them by messenger. Now. I don't care if you don't have a messenger— send someone in a cab, damn it! I can't believe we're paying him what we're paying him. Look. I've got someone here. Stay where you are. What's the number again?'' He took a pencil from his desk and jotted a telephone number on the bottom of a letter on his desk. ''Don't go away. I'll call you back in five minutes.''

Rao shook his head in disgust. ''Just now on the phone. This woman goes into minor surgery and wakes up bleeding—they can't stop the bleeding. She's a mess inside. Something happens that shouldn't have happened, something's gone wrong somewhere. There you have it. They say it has something to do with her. We say it has everything to do with them. What was the cause—a fuck-up by the doctor, or, in the parlance of the trade, her preexisting condition? She's in terrible shape. I visit her— she's home now—she can't stop crying. She cannot stop crying. Her husband's a bus driver for the city.

They have a little boy with these large, sad eyes who sits there and watches her. I know what happened, too. A fuck-up. The doctor fucked up. I know who he is—a doctor I know knows him well. He's a good doctor—I don't know what happened, but he fucked up. I can figure the medical side out myself. His mind wandered a bit—and his scalpel with it.''

Rao moved a pile of papers on his desk. "I'm sorry. I have to take care of this. Anything else you want to know?'' he said abruptly, then broke into laughter. "Quick! Quick! I'm a very busy man!''

"The business. What's it like?''

"Well, what do you want to know?''

"Whatever you want to tell me,'' I said.

"Big picture? Small picture?''

"Whatever you like.''

"Whatever I like. Whatever I like.'' Rao shrugged. "Well, you could say the woman who can't stop crying is the small picture. A lot of good that does her, right? The big picture?'' He shrugged again. "I don't know. In the big picture? Let's see. In the big picture—what am I? A minuscule part of—how would you describe it? The medical-care business. Which is how many hundreds of billion dollars a year? If I were doing products liability—which I have done—I would be a minuscule part of the economics of product distribution and selling, which is how many trillion dollars a year? If I did car-injury cases—which I have done—we're talking about how many injuries, how many hundreds of billions of dollars of economic loss a year to the entire society as a result of automobile accidents? The business?''

The phone was ringing again but Rao ignored it.

"The business you can figure out easily enough," he said. "We get a quarter to a third of what we recover. We have to pay for our own time until we do recover. So you're going to be very careful about what cases you take. You are going to watch your transactional costs, which include your time spent doing this or doing that. We're also going to settle at that point at which we think we can make the most money at the most propitious time—if we have to wait three years to get something, the insurance company has the money in a mutual fund, not us. I'm not telling you anything you don't already know. Those who look at us like we're rodents don't think about it that way, but they do the same goddamn thing, on their own scale. The public? The public believes in fairness. Well, what's fair for me isn't fair for you. The doctors? They're finally beginning to figure it out. What? Insurance. The invisible hand whacking them and the whole economy off. Insurance. Have you ever wondered what portion of our equity and bond markets is insurance money? What do you think? Twenty percent? Higher? Health insurance! So the big hospital complexes figure out they can insure themselves. Now they're merging. Then they'll buy an insurance company or two. They've already taken care of any antitrust problems with the Justice Department—they'll do it themselves—with, of course, the banks. Conglomerations. Conglomerated health care! The doctors? Maybe, at last, they'll finally see what's always been the case—they work for whoever is paying their customers' insurance."

Rao stopped. "Did you hear what I said?" he asked. "Because I'm right. The doctors just don't want to admit it. They work for and I mean *for*, whoever pays their customers'—their patients'—insurance. The government, a private company, the hospital they work for—what difference does it make who, finally, is paying it? Health-maintenance organizations—how about health-maintenance insurance companies! The sons of bitches withdrawing necessary care to save money. We're coming up with ways to sue them, too—we're going to bring down the entire make-money-at-the-expense-of-the-patient boondoggle. The doctors aren't going to stop it, so we will. We'll do it. But hey, please—don't take this as a harangue against insurance. It's there—part of nature, part of the nature of things. It's our pot of cash, too—I know that. I wouldn't be who I am without it —no question about it. Nor, might I add, would defense counsel of every stripe be where they are without us. We've all made each other rich."

Rao stood up and I did, too. He walked with me to the reception area. "So the big business corporations," he said, "get to the legislators—to do what? Cap—in one way or other—damages. Why? Less monetary incentive for us to sue. So, they think, their liability insurance will go down. Maybe it will, maybe it won't. I don't think it's going to go down, but I'm biased, right? It's not new, you know—the same thing, more or less, has been going on for years. So there's less potential money out there for us low-lifes. So? Finally, it's a business that rewards those who take what's there. You do what you have to do. What everyone else does? That's their game, not mine.

"This, though," Rao said, "I can assure you. There will still be injuries. Heinous, horrible injuries.

People will feel and will be aggrieved, and there will still be claims paid by insurance. To whose advantage is liability—ultimately? The more potential liability you have—it doesn't matter what kind of liability we're talking about, either—the more you have to insure, which means more money in the coffers of the insurance companies, which means the more there is to invest in the national and international financial markets, which, finally, help provide those very substantial livings for all those classmates of mine who are partners now at the Phillips Fineman Morrisons and Eliot & Brownwells of the world."

Two weeks later Frederick Singleton and I got together for lunch in his office on Broadway near City Hall. We ate in one of his firm's conference rooms, sushi ordered in from a restaurant on Fulton Street. He told me he didn't have much time but that he'd be happy to talk. Stocky and square-jawed, with short light brown hair, he spoke rapidly and openly, with a smile which bordered at times on a smirk. I asked him about himself. After graduating from law school, he said, he went to work for the city, defending personal-injury suits. He then worked three years with a plaintiffs' firm in the Woolworth Building. He was now a partner at a firm that did liability-insurance work and the head of the firm's medical-malpractice department. I asked him why he went from a defense practice to a plaintiffs' practice, then back to defense. He laughed out loud. "You know the old saying," he said. "I know how to keep the money in the safe."

"Doctors? Did you ask Tommy that, too?" he replied after I asked him what he thought about doctors. "Do I like them? Yeah," he said, nodding, "I like 'em. Definitely. Why, don't you? Doctors—they cool. Just regular folk, just trying to make a living like you and me. 'I said doctor—doctor!—Mr. M.D., can you tell me what's ailing me?' " he sang in a mimicking tone. "Tommy," he went on, "Tommy, I know, loves them. Loves them so much he sues their asses!" He picked up a piece of sushi with his chopsticks and ate it slowly. "Doctors? Let me give you an example. A cardiologist. His patient's a tool-and-die maker. He's worried that a stress test may precipitate a heart attack in this guy, so has him transferred to a hospital where they've got the facilities to do a catheterization. So a cardiologist there does a cath, which shows disease in one of the coronary vessels going to the posterior wall of the heart, and they decide the guy's not going to need an angioplasty or surgery. Unfortunately . . ."

Singleton smiled. "In my business, there is always an 'unfortunately.' Unfortunately, the cardiologist who performs the cath puts the catheter in wrong. Somehow there's an extravasation of blood, which this guy sees but can't comprehend—he should be contacting a vascular surgeon, but doesn't. He's off seeing other patients, two hours go by. The patient's blood pressure is dropping—he's got a horrible pain in his stomach. Finally, a vascular surgeon's called in. Before she—the vascular surgeon's a she—arrives, the cardiologist is assuming there's been a myocardial infarction—he's pumping the patient with Lasix. The vascular surgeon arrives, correctly diagnoses the problem as abdominal bleeding caused by the catheter. The patient, meanwhile"—Singleton paused and ate another piece of sushi—"the patient is bleeding to death. They get him into surgery, and the surgeon stops the bleeding. The guy stays in the hospital another week. Two months later, he's back to work, with no active disabilities. I agree. There's a lawsuit. The pain and suffering caused by the cardiologist's mistake. The pain and suffering of being brought to the brink of death. That's all the damages you've got—the guy needed a cath and he's functioning fine now. What do plaintiffs want? Seven million in pain and suffering. Oh, sure—no problem! But there is, I must admit, an alleged fact—a plaintiff's lawyer's *dream*. On the way to the O.R., the cardiologist and the surgeon are talking while the plaintiff's lying there, having lost all this blood, his stomach feeling like it's exploding. They think the guy's out cold, but, apparently, he's not—the plaintiff signs an affidavit that says the doctors were laughing. They're saying to each other that there's absolutely no way the guy's not gonna pop! Pop, incidentally," said Singleton, "is the word docs use to describe the act of death. You pop!"

"Do you think it's true?" I asked.

"How do I know if it's true?" Singleton shrugged, picking up another piece of sushi and swallowing it in one bite. "It's in the affidavit. It's what the plaintiff is going to testify to."

"What do the doctors say?"

"What the hell do you think they say?"

He sat back and snapped open the top of a can of Diet 7-Up, taking a long drink from it. "Your question about lawyers," he said. "I was on the phone this morning with a woman I worked with when I worked with the city who split New York after working a couple of years at Littan Taylor Gaillis. She lives in Denver now. I asked her how things were. She's a partner at one of the leading Denver firms. She said clients now tell *you*—in no uncertain terms—what *they* want. That's it. The idea of counsel, of giving advice? That you're supposed to advise the client when you're putting a deal together where the risks are—that this provision or that provision should be put into the deal in the event A, B, C, D, or E happens? She told me she had a client tell her not to worry about 'the nuances'—if something goes wrong, worry about it later. That's if anyone's still around. No one's staying at one place too long these days— *especially* clients. They want a document, a piece of paper, that's it. It's not a whole lot different from a form will. You go into the computer, pull out a prior deal, move provisions around, fill in the names of the parties, change some words here and there. Suggest a few more hours of work to put in, quote, the nuances, and you're told no, sorry. They'll go somewhere else. They're thinking why give the money to the lawyer, no matter how much it is. Keep it yourself."

Singleton paused, looking directly at me. "I can only speak for myself," he said, "but, in my opinion, things have changed *significantly* in the nine years I've been doing it. It's like that psychotic who killed those people on the Long Island Rail Road—what was his name? The psycho who tried his own case? One of the bailiffs—someone like that—said he wasn't all that bad, that, in fact, he was better in the courtroom

than many, if not most, of the lawyers he sees. That's
what I think's happened.'' Singleton moved his
tongue between his lower lip and his teeth. ''Everyone's a lawyer. Everyone now thinks like lawyers
think. Notice how often you hear the word 'transactional' these days? You didn't, not even five years
ago. Now everyone is using it. Invented''—he pointed
his thumb toward his chest—''by us liability types.
We are the original transactionals. That's good. I like
that. The original transactionals!''

Singleton wiped his fingers with a napkin, then finished his soda. He stood and walked over to his gray
suit jacket hung on another chair, pulling a cigarette
out of one of its pockets. ''I'm going to smoke,'' he
declared. ''I know we're not supposed to, but the
fuck if I'm going outside into twenty-degree weather
to do it. It's true,'' he went on, lighting his cigarette,
blowing the match out with the smoke he inhaled. He
was still standing. ''I'm not talking about criminal
law—which is booming. Though,'' he said, after taking a drag of his cigarette, ''I can see transactional
costs there, too. Take, for example, my clients. One,
in particular, underwrites medical-malpractice insurance. My client is obliged by contract to defend someone who's allegedly done a civil wrong—negligently
injured somebody. My client charges this someone
who allegedly negligently injured somebody X dollars
a year to insure him against any liability the legal
system may impose on him. My clients pay me—not
as much an hour as Salomon Brothers pays its outside
counsel, but I get paid well. In fact, in a way better,
because I don't have to deal with all the shit you have

to deal with with banks. My client has in-house counsel—a former partner of my firm is, in fact, head counsel. He's watching how much he's paying me at the same time he's figuring out how much of the cost of what he's paying me can be passed on to his insureds—the doctors—who, then, are figuring out how to pass that cost on to whoever needs, for example, a brain scan. There's a lawyer like Tommy Rao on the other side who knows he's got a five-million-dollar case—it can be any kind of case—if he can get me to a jury. But I also know he won't get me to a jury for at least three years, maybe five if I can delay it long enough, which I can do, and that he's paying money out of his pocket, and that if I offer him—round number—a million, he gets three hundred thousand dollars, roughly, tomorrow, which he can put into a T-bill, minimum six percent. If he waits five, he makes, with all the legislative limits on damages, how much? He's thinking that, I'm thinking that—you know it, I know it, and my client knows it. Transactional.''

Singleton sat down again, flicking the ash from his cigarette into the empty soda can. ''You take any legal problem,'' he said. ''Any form of negotiation. I once heard a very smart lawyer say that the art of negotiation is to make it easier for the other side to say yes rather than no. It's exactly right. The art of negotiation is to make it easier for the other side to say yes rather than no. So. What's Tommy get from me? Two million. My client knows how good Rao is—he doesn't want the litigation costs run up too high. We're not talking about a bogus case brought by a bogus lawyer where we'll spend money to smoke the fucking weasel out. We're also not talking about what I call the human factor. The plaintiff's lawyer, or your client, doesn't get what's happening transactionally, or does, and doesn't give a fuck—they want blood. So the lawyers on both sides give them what they want, which is blood. Never underestimate the revenge factor. People will spend a lot of money to get even. Let's assume we don't have any of that. Assume we have a plausible lawsuit—Tommy Rao wouldn't be bringing it if it weren't. Could Tommy have gotten us to the point where three million would have made it easier for us to say yes? I think so—but there will be other cases, and, knowing Tommy, he had other things on his mind. Tommy's thinking transactionally, too, in terms of his own goddamn business.''

''What do you think of plaintiffs' lawyers?'' I asked.

''Did you ask Tommy that?'' Singleton leaned over and put his cigarette out, pressing it into a plate. ''What do I think of plaintiffs' lawyers? Well, I once was one myself,'' he said, with a tone of thoughtfulness. ''I make money because of them. That's what I think of them. Other than that?'' He shrugged, then paused. ''A new associate of ours—a rookie—but very smart. We settle this shitass case for thirty thousand and she says, 'But our client didn't do anything wrong.' Wrong? Wrong? I told her right or wrong has nothing to do with it. If we thought—if the client thought—it was worth the money to litigate, we would have litigated. That sometimes you pay when you know the lawyer on the other side has figured out

you're going to pay no matter what the law is. The
law, I told her, is just another—and not always that
important—transactional consideration."

Singleton moved his chair back and put his feet up
on the conference table. He clasped his hands behind
his head. "Let me tell you what I think of plaintiffs'
lawyers," he said. "We'll let the facts speak for themselves. Guns are smuggled into Rikers Island—con-
victs bribe the guards. The smugglee, then, very
carefully, through a pillow, shoots himself—it's not
worth it to hurt yourself *too* seriously—on the surface
of his thigh. There are five, ten cases exactly like this.
Multimillion-dollar lawsuits. The city's negligent for
not preventing the guns from getting in—the city's
negligent because it didn't take adequate precautions
to make sure its inmates don't hurt themselves." Singleton put his feet back down, and leaned forward.
His steel-gray eyes were narrow. "Yes, yes—there's
an intervening-cause issue, and there's close to one
hundred percent contributory fault, but you take the
plaintiff as you find him, blah, blah, blah, blah, blah.
The bottom line? Who insures the city? You and I.
The deepest pocket on earth. You tell me," Singleton
asked, "what kind of person would write out a complaint in a case like that? While we're at it . . ."

He paused again. "Do you know what else gets me
hot? It's not as bad as it used to be, but you still see
it. This life-style crap. 'I'm really not a lawyer, I
am'—what? Every damn thing in the book. I'll say
this about doctors—can you imagine, you go to a doctor, and the doctor tells you that he really hates being
a doctor, that what he really is, is the lead singer in

a band, the Dog Dirts? The fucker would be sued for malpractice.''

Singleton stood up and straightened his shoulders. ''Ever notice how it—it sort of takes over? Like a disease?''

He put his jacket back on and then sat down again, crossing his legs, slouched in his chair. ''This was three days ago. This past Monday. There was a sale—one of those cheap shoe stores on Nassau. A little after lunchtime. I ask to try on three pairs of shoes. The guy—he was from Bangladesh. I could tell by the accent. I know doctors from Bangladesh. He spoke with a Bengali accent. You know—not that choppy way the A-rabs talk—but the choppiness with the singsong, that jive singsong that drives you crazy. This guy was very dark—black, really. He goes downstairs, comes back up, he's pissed off, he hates his job, he hates me—have you noticed the entire city's a bunch of immigrants who hate their jobs and hate you for making them do them? Of course, the shoes don't fit right. I say, as politely as I can, I'm sorry, but these don't fit right. Suddenly there's this attitude. Oilyhead says to me, 'What-a do-a you-a mean-a none-of-a these-are-a right?' I ask him—I'm trying to be polite—is there any problem. Do you know what he says to me? He says, 'You-are-a the problem.' 'I'm the problem?' I say, I must admit''—Singleton put his hand up—''a tiny bit perturbed. 'Why am I the problem?' I ask. 'I really don't see why I'm a problem, sir.'

''Well, the 'sir' sets the guy into orbit. He's got a build to him—five-ten, maybe, heavyset, a thick neck. His carotid artery starts pumping up and down. 'Fuck you!' he says—no singsong to it, either. This guy is telling me to get fucked! 'What did you say?' I asked. 'Fuck you,' he says again. 'Well, go fuck yourself,' I say. He then says to me—quite defiantly, actually—back into singsong, 'Why-a don't-you-a leave-out-of the-store-a.' I say no. I tell him I have no intention of leaving out of the store-a. I tell him I'd like to look at more shoes. The guy goes nuts! You can see it—he wants to punch me. 'Please sir, please,' I say—I've got my voice as low as I can get it. 'Please, sir, please, please, please, please, sir—right here. Hit me. Take your fist and hit me. Here. In the face'— I've got my face right next to his—'please hit me as hard as you can. Please, sir—make my life—hit me. Please!' Suddenly he's getting real nervous. 'Please, sir, please, sir, hit me, please, sir,' I say. 'Please, sir, please—and, sir, please, after you hit me, call the police. Please!' There's another sales guy there, a Caribbean type. I like those guys. At least you can talk to them. He comes over and asks me—he's trying to chill me out—to leave. I ask for the owner. He says the owner isn't there. I ask him, 'By the way, does your friend have his green card in order?' Ka-*boom*! 'Boy,' I say, 'wouldn't the Immigration and Naturalization Service like to hear about an assault and a battery in a shoe store that's probably a front for drugs?' Ka-*boom*! Ka-*boom-boom-boom*!'"

Singleton took a pack of Marlboro Lights from his suit jacket, placed it on the conference table, pulled a cigarette from it, lit it, inhaled, then, turning his face to the side, exhaled a mouthful of smoke.

"By now," he said, "beads of perspiration are forming on Bong-a-la-desh-ee's forehead. I stay there a moment or two more, I don't say anything, letting the tension build. Then I walk out, and say as I go by him, my voice as soft as I can make it, 'Fuck you, you fucking illegal, fuck fucking you!' "

Cerriere's Answer

WE DON'T HAVE TO MEET CERRIERE FOR AN-
other forty-five minutes," Martha Tharaud
said to me as we stood on the corner of Maiden
Lane and Pearl, "so I thought, since it's such a beautiful day, we'd take a walk around the neighborhood
first." She turned and pointed. "The Federal Reserve," she said. "A replication of the Palazzo
Strozzi in Florence. The Strozzis were Florence's
bankers. The fifteenth century. I think that was when
Dante wrote the *Divine Comedy*—I don't exactly re-
call. Beneath it—I'm not sure if you know this—are
small cells, like jail cells. There are thousands of tons
of gold in them. A quarter of the world's monetary
gold is seventy-five feet beneath sea level, beneath
Liberty, Nassau, Maiden Lane, and William streets.
Those pieces of sculpture in front of the Fed are Lou-

ise Nevelsons. Across the street from the Fed, the tall white marble-looking building . . .''

"The Chase Bank building," I said.

"I was wondering if they were going to rename themselves Chemical Chase, or Chase Chemical, after the merger I guess it's now just Chase. The Rockefellers' bank. Who do you think had more money, the Strozzis or the Rockefellers? I'm pretty sure the Strozzis didn't make their money in oil. Those magnificent huge, round black-and-white shapes made of aluminum, by Dubuffet, in front of the building—I try to go by them as often as I can. They're really quite wonderful."

Tharaud then turned in the other direction, suggesting that we walk down to the river. The late-February afternoon was bright and windy, with large clouds floating across the sky. "There's a touch of spring in the air, a touch of April, she said. "I love this breeze." With slightly stooped shoulders, Tharaud walked quickly but cautiously, speaking slowly. She was in her early sixties, and one of the preeminent labor lawyers of her generation. There was about her a combination of sharpness and composure—she seemed to know at all times what she wanted to say, and listened attentively to what you were saying. Trim, of medium height, she was wearing a dark green trench coat over a navy-blue suit, an oval-shaped jade brooch pinned to one of its collars. Her hair, silver-white, was combed back and clasped by a barrette made of the same jade as her brooch, which, she said, she bought in Mexico in the fifties. "You know, I've never *not* worked down here," she said. "I've worked down here for over forty years.

I'd never thought of it before now, but the Fed, you know, has changed, too. Everyone in my father's day, all they would talk about was gold. I can remember hearing—this was over on Broad Street. A lawyer—his name was Arthur. Arthur Pendleton III. Pendleton & Strong—Arthur's grandfather was the founding partner. By the time they got to Arthur, the blood was a bit thin. Arthur opposed—vehemently—the National Labor Relations Act, the minimum wage, unemployment compensation, Social Security. This was in fifty-three, fifty-four. The legislation then, you have to remember, hadn't been around even twenty years yet. Arthur would say—it sounds almost quaint now—that his constitutional rights had been violated. He used to lift his finger and pronounce, 'They are in violation of my constitutional rights!' He had the most horrible, scratchy voice.''

We waited at Maiden Lane and Water Street for the light to change. "Arthur"—Tharaud smiled—"even thought the Federal Reserve was unconstitutional. He'd obsess about it in his own thin-lipped way. He didn't like me. I was a colored girl. A girl first, but, close behind, colored. Back then, we were colored people. Orientals. I'm told it's bad manners to use the word now. Levantines"—the light changed and we crossed Water Street—"that was another thing we were, Levantines. You know, darkies. Then, of course, we were Communists, Bolsheviks—every one of us. Lenin was a Jew, of course—which, of course, he wasn't. I shouldn't have said every one of us—where," Tharaud asked, stopping on the sidewalk after we crossed, touching my arm, "is my head? All of us were not only flaming Bolsheviks, we were rich international bankers as well. The contradiction," she said, then sighed, "seems to have escaped Arthur. Not that he would have cared. Did you know that *I* was responsible for the First World War? It's too bad Arthur didn't live to see today. The Fed's now a big-time bond player—in addition, of course, to controlling the economy by determining the rates Arthur's banker grandchildren can buy and sell and make all their money at."

We walked to the corner of Maiden Lane and South Street. On the other side of the street, past a small parking lot, was the East River. Across the river was Brooklyn Heights. "It's funny how you remember things," Tharaud went on. "Nineteen fifty-three —it seems like eons ago! Arthur D. Pendleton III. I'd just graduated from law school and had been on the job only a month or so—it was October, I remember, a chilly, gray October day. Lewis took me with him to a bargaining session for the maritime people— there were some old-school dock workers back then —Steve DePietro, Jack 'Moho' Mohoney, from when this island was really a port." I asked where the docks had been. "Down here," Tharaud said, waving her hand toward the harbor. "Up the Hudson, too. What is now Battery Park City was docks. It was after the war that things changed. In the fifties a number of piers burned. Arson. The city bought them out. I worked with Lewis Harris back then. Lewis was a great lawyer.

"You know," Tharaud said, stopping, "why don't we go back? There's a fast-food place on Pearl, they have a few tables—you can sit and talk and no one will bother you. We'll be closer to where we'll be meeting Cerriere. I don't want to walk too far." We walked back up Maiden Lane. "Lewis was a phenomenal lawyer," she continued. "Lewis Harris helped change considerably—and for the better—the living standards of hundreds of thousands of people. I remember one time we were in the middle of a contract negotiation, when Arthur looks at me, then looks at Lewis, and then starts in on Trotsky. Can you imagine that? Trotsky! He had this curled upper lip, Arthur —God rest his soul—his curled lip starts twitching, like this . . ." Tharaud stopped and held her upper lip, moving it up and down. "The very *thought* of Trotsky had him in paroxysms! He asks Lewis—I, by the way, did not exist—which, Arthur never realized, made me into a very dangerous person. You make someone invisible and you make them into a very dangerous person. Arthur asked Lewis if he knew that Trotsky was living in the Bronx—that he wasn't in Holy Russia right before . . . Arthur couldn't even *say* the word revolution! 'Did you know that Trotsky's real name wasn't Trotsky?' he asked Lewis, this very mean look in his eyes—I can see it as though it were yesterday. 'Trotsky's *real* name was Leon Davidowitch Bronstein. Bronstein!' He spit the word out—I'm not exaggerating. There was spittle coming from his mouth. He pronounced 'stein' 'stine,' not 'steen.' God, what an unpleasant human being.

"Now, this street has changed," Tharaud said, nodding in both directions, as we came again to Pearl Street. "The place we're going to, Ying's"—she gestured in the direction of the Brooklyn Bridge—"is over here. Years ago it was a tailor's. This glass monstrosity"—she nodded in the other direction—

"was built in the late fifties. Copeland Gerard was one of the original tenants. They used to be up and around the corner, on Cedar, near William. I love Cedar. It still has the look of a dark canyon. Your old-fashioned, downtown one-way street. We used to be on Liberty near Nassau. Lewis used to say, 'Liberty begins and ends with the Federal Reserve.' I have never forgotten it. I remember it every time I see the Fed—which has been nearly every day of my life for the last forty years. Copeland Gerard, by the way, is a very good firm. If I needed a management firm, that's who I'd hire."

We walked into Ying's. We ordered Cokes—Tharaud, also, a serving of white rice—paid, and sat at a Formica table near a window facing Pearl Street. "I like the name—Ying's," Tharaud said. "Up the yin-yang—that's what it reminds me of. One of my younger partners says it all the time. He's from Wisconsin, this young man. Superior, Wisconsin. Way up north, on Lake Superior, near the Minnesota border, not far from Duluth. He's always talking about Wisconsin. Mostly how cold the winters are. He's always saying that, historically, it's one of our most progressive states. To which I add that, indeed, it has been, and is—and that it's also the state that gave us Senator Joseph McCarthy. Up the yin-yang"—Tharaud smiled—"right? My partner's great third cousin—or something like that—was, of all people, Thorstein Veblen. I want to say something about that, but, for just a moment—because that's all he's worth—the former senator from Wisconsin. A lawyer, you know, McCarthy. A lawyer whose lawyer was Roy Cohn." I asked Tharaud if she'd known Cohn. "Yes, I knew him," she said. "A very famous man in his time, Roy Cohn. During the Simpson thing the younger lawyers in our office were talking about how famous Johnnie Cochran is. Johnnie Cochran's fame is—I was tempted to say was—nothing, nothing compared to Roy Cohn's. I asked them what they knew about Cohn. All they knew was that he was secretly gay but openly contemptuous of homosexuals. Contemptuous isn't a strong enough word—not when you're talking about Roy Cohn. He had very powerful friends, Mr. Cohn. An insider's insider's insider—he had something on everybody. Well, he was—whore isn't the right word. He certainly was a whore. Pimp is more like it. Every species has its perfect flower. The perfect lawyer pimp. A footnote of a footnote of a footnote of a footnote—he doesn't even deserve that. Boy, he hurt a lot of people."

Tharaud lowered her voice. "Did you notice the girl who took our order?" she asked. "It's a game I play. You can figure out the entire political and economic picture by looking at one single employment relationship. Go ahead," she insisted. "Take a look at her."

I turned and took a quick look. "She's how old, do you think?" Tharaud asked. "Twenty-two? Twenty-three? Chinese, I'd say—but why not be honest about it? I can't distinguish among Asians very well. I assume she's Chinese. Very pretty but very frail—not even five feet. She can't weigh more than ninety pounds. Speaks English with no trace of an accent. Think she was born here? I have no idea.

Where do you think she lives? Queens, probably. I wonder if she understands her polygraph protection rights.''

Tharaud was referring to small posters behind the counter that summarized an employee's statutory rights under various federal and state laws, including the federal Polygraph Protection Act and New York State's Workers' Compensation Act.

"Of course," Tharaud said, "it doesn't matter. Since there's no union, if Ying's wants to fire her, Ying's can fire her. How about if she slips and falls on some noodles one of her fellow workers spilled on the floor and fractures her knee? Or her skull? She fractures her skull. She's clearly an employee. Do you think she'd file a comp claim? Do you think that if she filed a comp claim it would upset Mr. Ying? But let us say—in the world of the hypothetical, of course—let us say, nevertheless, that she wishes to exercise her statutory rights. How, then, does she go about it? Where does she find a workers' comp lawyer? Maybe that man in the brown double-breasted suit sitting over there''—Tharaud moved her eyes across the room—''maybe he's a comp lawyer. Should we ask him? I really shouldn't be such a snob. How do I know? Maybe he manages life-insurance accounts in one of those buildings around the corner on John Street. Maybe he's an over-the-counter trader in one of those old buildings on Broad Street. What do you think this girl is making an hour? That we know. Minimum wage. Five dollars, roughly, an hour, forty hours a week—two hundred dollars a week, eight hundred a month, ninety-six hundred a year, before taxes. That gives her about seventy-five hundred dollars for food, rent, a night on the town, health insurance, and, if she has children—do you think she has children? I didn't see a wedding band, but who knows? If she has children, who is taking care of them? Not day-care—day-care costs over five dollars an hour. Maybe she's married and her husband's an institutional investor—how do I know? They had a good year last year. Maybe she's doing this so she can be among the people."

Tharaud finished her Coke. She hadn't touched the rice at all. "About a mile, a mile and a half, from here, there are sweatshops, you know. Not facsimiles, either—I'm talking about bona fide sweatshops. A few blocks away from the courts and One Police Plaza. No different from what you had a hundred years ago. Women. Some of them have been kidnapped. A form—what am I saying, a form? Indentured servitude. That's what it is. These women are kidnapped or sold, then shipped here, then hired out to make clothes or forced into prostitution, to pay off the perverts—the depraved, evil perverts—who smuggled them here. A few blocks from your très chic SoHo restaurants, some of which—Savoy, for instance—I frequent. Compared to them, I'd say this girl is of a higher class—if, by class, we mean the amount of economic control you have over your work. I'd say she has more economic control over her work than a woman her age in a sweatshop, wouldn't you?"

Tharaud stopped, silent for a moment, positioning her body sideways in her chair and looking out the window. "Why don't we get out of here and walk some more," she turned to me and said. "We've still got a few more minutes before we meet Cerriere.

We're meeting him at the Dean & Deluca's near Hanover Square. The light this time of day there—it's what I imagine the Viennese Belle Epoque cafés to have been like. It's a reconversion of the old Cocoa Exchange building—twenty-foot-high ceilings, large ceiling fans, large windows. As for Cerriere—well, you'll see for yourself."

We walked on Pearl over to Wall Street, and then down Wall to the East River. I asked Tharaud how she thought Wall Street had changed. "Eighty-two, eighty-three, to eighty-seven—the four to five years in the eighties when the Federal Treasury was looted—that was the big change," she said. "The Boom. A lot of these high-rise office buildings—a number of them went into bankruptcy. The Seaport —none of that was here at the end of the seventies. It used to be just a market. Over on Broad, on Stone, near Beaver, two blocks from the Stock Exchange, the grand buildings of the twenties boom—some of them are empty, they look like ruins. Although there may be more money down here now, sheer quantity, in real dollars, than ever before, at least in my lifetime. They've started building again. The money has to go somewhere. Such strange times! I'm glad I'm at the end of my career. I remember when we used to talk about economies of scale—now it's speed. Economies of speed! My partner, Veblen's grandcousin or great-grandcousin, he was surprised I knew who Thorstein Veblen was. Of course I know who Thorstein Veblen was. He'd be like who today? There's really no one like Thorstein Veblen today. He was the one, you know, who came up with the term 'conspicuous consumption,' a hundred years ago. It's still in the language—I heard it used the other day. Veblen believed—he was sure of it—that capitalism couldn't survive without being managed from the top. That it would destroy itself and everyone with it. I asked my partner what he thought of cousin Thorstein. Now this is a very socially aware young man, a very good lawyer—I'm very fond of him. Do you know what he said?"

Tharaud smiled. " 'Cousin Thorstein was primitive.' Primitive! At first I thought, no—I was about to argue with him—when I realized he was right. Even Keynes is primitive now. It would be interesting to ask one of the millions of bachelor's or master's degrees in business administration out there if they've ever read anything by Keynes. An old friend who teaches economics at Princeton—he's about to retire—told me, not long ago, that there are collections of Keynes's writings that have *never* been taken out of the Princeton library since they were published in the early seventies. This is Princeton. Imagine bringing up Keynes in one of these megahouses—some of them with more money than most countries in the world. You'd have more luck talking about—who knows? At some point one gets the idea, doesn't one?"

We walked on South Street, then turned on Old Slip. "But," Tharaud said, putting her hand over her eyes to protect them from the sun, "you want to know what I think about lawyers, not about John Maynard Keynes's books in the Princeton library. I'm probably, actually, not that bad a person to ask. How many women attorneys are there in my generation? Not many. Lawyers. God, I don't know. Let me think. What, now, as I approach the end of the journey, do I think of lawyers? God, I'm sounding almost wistful.''

"Have you been aware of the fact that you're a woman?''

"Have I been aware of the fact that I'm a woman?'' Tharaud suddenly bristled. "What do you think? Have I been aware of the fact that I'm a woman.'' There was a long silence. "I really don't know what would make you ask a question like that. What it's like to be a woman in this business! I'll tell you what it's like. I can't even remember all the indignities. It makes a difference now that there are more of us—but, at another level, it only means that the indignities change form, and in some instances even multiply. A whole lot of women disappear in this business. Where do they go? Is anyone trying to figure out what happens to them? Why not? Tell me, why not?''

We came to Hanover Square. Tharaud said that she would like to sit a few minutes before meeting Cerriere. We found a bench in the Square. "Theodore Dreiser,'' she said, after we'd sat in silence for a while. "Dreiser said the favorite drama of the American people is the story of a murder trial. Nineteen twenty-five he said it. During *that* big-money boomtime. Notice he said the favorite drama, not the *real* drama. The real drama? No one wants to talk about it. Work. Wages. Hours. Conditions of employment. Employment! Listen closely to what people talk about—it's what people talk about almost all the time. Let me tell you this about law. One of the fundamental legal relationships in any society—as fundamental as the relationship between the state and who the state deems its criminals—is the employment contract. It is certainly as fundamental as a commercial transaction, wouldn't you say? Everyone has one, or wants one, or for some reason or other will never be able to have one, or keep one, right? What's more fundamental than that? Why the big secret? Explain to me, will you—what's the big secret? Why not Court TV on how we are employed? 'What we do unto others and do unto ourselves.' "

Tharaud turned and looked straight at me. "I've got a word of wisdom for you," she said. "Here's a bit of wisdom for you. Pardon me if I sound patronizing. But you want to know what I think? I think the truth eventually will be revealed. That's what I think. Eventually the truth will be revealed. Sound like a preacher, don't I? Well, it's true. Eventually it will. Lawyers, the best of us, we know how to reveal it, too. I've always liked the verb we use—ferret. Lawyers know how to ferret out what's true from what appears to be true. Truth exists somewhere between what you can prove and can't—that we know. In due course, what can be proved and what cannot be proved will be clear to us all. I believe it."

Tharaud stopped. Her voice softened. "I apologize for my little fit of anger," she said, then paused. "I get carried away sometimes. I apologize." She looked at her watch. "One last piece of wisdom, and then we've got to go and see Cerriere. It's something that you don't realize until you're older. Most people are dim. I don't mean mean or stupid—although there are plenty of dim people who are also mean and stupid—I mean something else. A thickness, a thickheadedness, a dullness. When you're younger you say to yourself, who am I to presume someone is dull? But the older you get, you realize you've wasted so much time, so much time lost. No appreciation of subtlety, of beauty. That's what it is. That, finally, is what it is. To know anything about beauty, you have to take the trouble to learn. Most lawyers are like most everyone else—they don't take the trouble to learn anything other than what puts money into their pockets. I know it sounds like a cliché, but it isn't even a cliché anymore—no one talks about it anymore. What happens is, one day the dimwits wake up in a 'what-is-life-really-about?' stupor, but it's too late, it's already over, so they try to bring you down into their misery. It happens over and over again—every generation, the same thing happens. How many lawyers do you know who think of themselves as sophisticates, cosmopolitans, when, in reality, they don't know very much about very much at all. In the scheme of things it's all so silly, but, in the scheme of things, there are a lot of people hurt by it, really hurt. I'm not sure, either, what you can do about it, other than protect yourself, protect what you believe in, those whom you love. I'm really not sure there's a whole lot more you can do about it.''

You're not curious what it is we've just settled?'' Cerriere asked, putting his copies of the settlement agreement into his briefcase. "Didn't Martha tell you how much is going into the coffers of Tharaud Tineman & Conway? Tell him, Martha. Go on, tell him.''

Tharaud smiled. "Robert's client—more precisely, a managerial employee of Robert's client—has what my male colleagues call a 'pussy obsession.' Isn't that what you'd call it, Robert?"

"Precisely, Martha. That's precisely what it was."

"Robert's client—but why get graphic? Robert's firm was smart enough not to play hardball on this one. Robert"—Tharaud turned to me—"is the rising labor and employment law star at Villard Steinman, you know. Old Judge Villard—the judge would have been proud of Robert. Robert's devotion to his clients is touching."

"Martha really doesn't like me very much," Cerriere said, turning to Tharaud. "Do you, Martha?"

"That's not true, Robert," Tharaud said. "What makes you think that? I like you, Robert—it's your clients I don't like."

"Don't think that Martha's not liking me hasn't been a problem either—professionally, I mean," Cerriere said. "I don't know if you're aware how much power Martha has. Martha Tharaud puts her name on a complaint and Tharaud Tineman & Conway gets two hundred fifty thousand, just like that. Like magic! Isn't that right, Martha?"

"Your problem, Robert, is you're too sensitive," Tharaud said. "You must remember that it's nothing personal. In fact"—she turned to me again—"compared to his partners, Robert's a splendid fellow. You've probably never had the pleasure of meeting the senior partner in the labor and employment law section of Judge Villard's great firm, James C. Halley. Though I'm worried about Jimmy. The last time I saw him he looked a bit—what's the word—large? A little like Warren Harding. But I mustn't forget that Jimmy has strong genes. 'Of humble beginnings, James C.

Halley, of Akron, Ohio.' A child of the Great Depression. Jimmy will tell you all about it. 'The bur-
dens of the smokestacks at dawn and at dusk.' "

"You surprise me, Martha," Cerriere said, standing up to take his suit jacket off. He fixed his tie, then
ran his hands through his thinning brown hair. He
had hazel eyes, which, when he wasn't speaking, took
on an aggressive, edgy expression. His voice was quick
and sharp. "I thought you'd be on the side of the
large, Martha," he said, moving his chair back from
the small table to accommodate his tall, thin frame,
then sitting down. "I don't know how familiar you
are with the kind of work we do," he said to me. "Or
I should say the kind that Martha does. Martha's one
of a kind, you know. Hiring, suspension, retirement,
discipline, promotion, harassment, firing—you name
it, Tharaud Tineman & Conway brings it."

"Why is getting fired last on your list, Robert?"
Tharaud asked.

"Don't interrupt me, Martha," Cerriere said. "I
wasn't finished speaking. It's not very good manners,
you know. May I finish?"

Cerriere looked at me again. "Martha's modest.
No one in this business is more generous than Martha.
She'll sue anyone! The greatest equal-opportunity
lawyer alive!"

"What Robert is . . ."

"May I finish, Martha? Please?" Cerriere paused
a few seconds. "May I talk now, Martha? Is that all
right with you?"

Tharaud was silent.

"Thank you," Cerriere said, "thank you very
much." He paused again. "Now, where was I? Oh,

yes. Martha's generosity. Not only large, horrible corporations," said Cerriere. "No sir-ee—not Martha. It doesn't matter who you are. A small mom-and-pop business. Schools—Martha *loves* to sue schools. Universities—any place of education. Government. How much have you made suing the government, Martha? Conservative estimate. Ten million? Look! She won't answer. I'll bet it's more than ten."

Tharaud was sitting back in her chair, a vacant look on her face. Cerriere stared at her, bemused. "Look at her!" he said. "You don't like this, do you, Martha?" Tharaud looked at him without any expression on her face. "I have to admit," Cerriere said to me, "I'm somewhat surprised by Martha's comment about Halley's fat. Fat is not supposed to count, is it, Martha? Every once in a while it does, though. In fact, there's a recent California court of appeals case—you'll like this. A prosecuting attorney wants to remove three women as jurors in a murder case. One's obese, one's hair is braided, the third's obese with braided hair and wears a dashiki. The prosecutor says he doesn't like young, fat, counterculture sisters—he probably would have liked to have thrown in lesbian, but that would have created problems— and says they don't like him because, sensitive people that they are, they pick up on his negative vibe. Upheld. In California, a juror's appearance or dress may be grounds for peremptory removal. A person— notice, Martha, that I said 'person'—very fat and poorly groomed might not be in the mainstream of people's thinking. Something like that. There's no need to put too fine a point on it."

Cerriere laughed out loud. "Just look at her!" he

said, nodding at Tharaud. "Relax, Martha. You'll have your chance. I'm just not finished yet. You know, don't you, what she's probably thinking?" Cerriere asked me. "The Disabilities Act. Right, Martha?" Tharaud didn't answer. "Look," Cerriere said, smiling. "Look at her. She's getting pissed off! You can see it in her face. They all get like that. You should hear her partner—Mike 'I-am-the-great-grandson-of-a-poor-Hibernian-potato-eater' Conway. At least Halley really grew up working-class. Conway's just full of shit. You should hear him. He's *gooooood*. Brings an Irish tear to your eye. The perfect touch of brogue. You should hear him say 'discrimination'—he, like, lolls the word around his tongue in this deep, *deeeeeeep* voice. I'm not very good at imitations," Cerriere said. "*Dee-scrimmm-in—ay-shun*. 'How about if you're a faggot or a lesbo, Mike?' "

"You're married, aren't you, Robert?" Tharaud asked.

Cerriere looked at her. "Yes, Martha," he said, "I'm married."

"What's your wife do?"

"My wife's a management consultant, Martha."

"Does she work for someone?"

"Ah! I get it! Martha's so subtle! Never transparent, not Martha! Has my wife ever been sexually harassed? Good, Martha."

"We have clients like your wife—what's her name, did you tell me her name, Robert? At one of those meetings so popular these days in American business, management sitting around earnestly . . ."

"Earnestly?" Cerriere said.

"That's what I said, Robert. Earnestly. They're like you are, Robert. The mission, the values, the vision of the company—it's no joking matter. While the help—including some of the jokers sitting around the table—are terrified of being fired. Simple question, Robert, which you need not answer—but what if, let's say, one of those fellows in management who's hired your wife's firm that day . . . By the way, Robert, is your wife an employee or an independent contractor?"

"Cut the shit, Martha. We know what you're going to say."

"What if nice-guy management asks your wife—how old is your wife, Robert? Early- or mid-thirties, like you are—I'm sure she's very sexy, too. Men like to look at her, right? What if one of those nice fellows at the meeting asks your wife what color her panties are? Cause of action, Robert?"

Cerriere rubbed his eyes with his fingers, then shook his head wearily, before looking directly at Tharaud.

"I haven't upset you," Tharaud asked, "have I, Robert? Have I upset you? These things, of course, do not happen. Not to graduates of the Wharton School. But"—Tharaud sat up in her chair—"let's say, hypothetically of course, that it does happen. Of course it would never *really* happen—but if it did, and were to continue—like in this case we just settled. By the way," Tharaud said to me, "Robert didn't tell you—did you, Robert?—that by not litigating this case he saved his client, oh, maybe, a half million dollars. That's about right, isn't it, Robert? What if," she asked Cerriere, "that nice fellow asked your wife if she gets moist between her legs when she's around him, Robert?''

"Enough, Martha," Cerriere said.

"How about, 'I know you're thinking of me when you're fucking your husband,' who would be you, wouldn't it, Robert?''

"That's it," Cerriere said. "I'm not going to sit here and listen to this bullshit."

There was a long, tense silence. Dean & Deluca's was almost empty, except for a man and a woman having coffee at a table across the café. A young man was mopping the floor near where we were sitting.

"We should move," Tharaud finally said, her voice softer. "The smell of the disinfectant is too much."

"I'm going to go," Cerriere said. "It's not like we can get into a fistfight." He started to smile.

"It's always been an advantage of mine," Tharaud said with a laugh. "Robert," she said to me, "is referring to a famous fight between a partner of mine and a partner of his. Over on Theatre Alley, across from City Hall Park. It really is an alley—between Beekman and Anne. It must have been the alley behind the theaters that were on Park Row—Park Row was a theater district at the turn of the century. A real punch-out. I'm trying to remember when that was."

"Twenty years ago," Cerriere said.

"That sounds about right," said Tharaud. "The city was close to bankrupt. I can't even remember what it was about."

"No one knows what it was about," said Cerriere. "When I started at Villard, everyone used to talk

about it. Syrett"—he said to me—"that's Martha's
partner, kicked the shit out of Marrow, my partner.
Marrow is an asshole, but so is Syrett. You can't
deny, Martha, that Syrett is an asshole."

"Syrett is an asshole," Tharaud said. "He lost
five or six teeth. He had to have a bridge put in his
mouth, then dentures. Roger's known to take them
out at partners' meetings. A kind of reminder to all
of us of his devotion to the firm."

"There's a firm picture from around then," Cerriere said, shaking his head. "Marrow's got a band-
age over his nose and his jaw's broken. Syrett literally
busted his chops. Marrow's got this ugly, crooked
nose—his jaw's unhinged. It moves around when he
talks. We have clients who take a look at him and
can't stop laughing. He looks like fucking Franken-
stein."

"We really should move," Tharaud said. "The
smell of whatever this young man is mopping—it really is too much for me."

We moved to a table on the other side of the café,
tiptoeing over the wet floor. "So Martha tells me
you're here to find out what we do," Cerriere said
after we'd seated ourselves at another table. "I'm a
neophyte. Martha was practicing before the Wagner
Act was passed."

"Not quite," Tharaud said. "I was opposed to it,
though, because it gave too much power to the
government."

There was another silence.

"Do you ever wonder what that young man's life
is like?" Tharaud asked.

"Here we go," said Cerriere. "So, tell us, Martha, what is his life like?"

Tharaud looked down at her watch. "My friend here wants to know what we do, Robert. Why don't we get on with it."

Cerriere was rubbing his long fingers again into his eyes. "Why don't we do this," he said slowly. "You say what you think it is I do, and then I'll say what it is I think you do."

"Fair enough," Tharaud said, and then was silent.

"Beware. Martha Tharaud's thinking," Cerriere said.

"Essentially . . ."

"Essentially," Cerriere cut in. "Earnestly, essentially—good, Martha."

"What Robert essentially does is advise his clients how to fire people without incurring liability."

Cerriere started to interrupt, but Tharaud stopped him. "You agreed to let me say what I think it is you do, Robert, didn't you? That is what I'm doing. Let me do it. Then you can say whatever you want."

Cerriere, arms folded, sat back in his chair.

"I don't know," Tharaud went on, "if you've ever seen the reports Robert's firm puts out. They write handbooks. Newsletters."

"We don't do that, Martha," Cerriere said.

"How to fire people," Tharaud said. "Not kids who work for Burger King or this young man who's mopping the floor. They get fired and that's that. Off they go—wherever they go. No, Robert advises his clients how to fire the Roberts of the world."

"You know, Martha," Cerriere said, "you amaze me. Simply fucking amaze me."

"They have all sorts of new words for it, too. 'Deselected.' That's one I heard for the first time the other day. Deselected. 'Sorry, we have to deselect you.' Then there's 'decruited.' 'Excessed' is another. 'Surplussed.' Isn't that wonderful? 'You are being surplussed.' Then, of course, there's riffing. R-I-F-ing. 'Reduction in force.' Robert's a reduction-in-force-er. He enforces reduction. You've got to be strong to do that!"

Cerriere started to speak but Tharaud cut him off again. "Are you, or aren't you, going to let me finish, Robert?" Cerriere was silent. Tharaud took a deep breath and continued. "I remember after the war— I was still in high school—the words used were 're-deployment,' 'reconversion.' Now it's downsize. Job security, economic security—kids these days don't even know what they mean. It's like World War II to them—'there were atomic bombs dropped on Japan and there was job security.' Though, of course, there was never really that much. Anyway, it's history now. Robert and his partners figured out how—I should say their clients paid them enormous amounts of money to figure out how—to get half the number of people to work twice as hard, with three, four times as much output. You pay a certain few a lot of money . . ."

"That's it," Cerriere said.

"Pay a certain few a lot of money to cut your work force in half, then eliminate half—two-thirds, if you can—of the rest. Downsize—doesn't it really mean eliminate? Then why not just say 'eliminate,' Robert?

Why not get rid of it all? Pensions, health insurance —go all the way! Take control of the government and eliminate—eliminate all those inefficient obligations the government imposes on bosses. The beauty of it being, the more people you eliminate, the higher your equity. Up it goes! Up, up, up, up, up!''

''You can't even hear yourself, can you, Martha —you're fucking pontificating.''

''Robert can't stand ideas,'' Tharaud said. ''Can you, Robert?''

''Do you know what?'' Cerriere turned to me. His voice was even again. ''Martha is right. She's right. I am convinced. Martha has convinced me. From now on, I'm going to advise my clients to keep employing people they *don't* need, to make sure that the people they *don't* need are happy and content and have a high sense of self-esteem and *don't* feel victimized. That they should pay them five times . . . Why not ten? Pay them ten times what they're worth because they're nice, decent people.''

''Are you finished interrupting me yet?'' asked Tharaud.

''I am finished interrupting you, Martha. I am sorry I interrupted you. You can finish. In fact, I'm looking forward to it. Just one more thing—it'll take just a second. In Bosnia. Allegations—of course, only allegations. A detailed indictment. A Bosnian Serb. Forced a Muslim prisoner—I'm sorry to be so graphic here, but the law, after all, can be a very graphic business. A Bosnian Serb forced a Muslim prisoner to bite off the testicles of another prisoner who wouldn't stop screaming. Well, he stopped screaming. Don't

cringe, Martha! It's the real world! Pol Pot—you remember Pol Pot, don't you, Martha? Pol Pot ordered
everyone who wore glasses murdered. I wear glasses
when I read—I'm sure you do, too, Martha. I don't
think either of us would have fared too well under
Pol Pot's executive mandate, now, would we have?''

Tharaud began to gather the papers scattered on
the table, putting them into her briefcase. Cerriere
leaned close to her and laughed. ''Mop Boy!'' he said,
nodding toward the counter, where the young man
who'd been mopping the floor was talking with another employee.

Tharaud stopped and stared at him.

''Mop Boy!'' Cerriere said again. ''I must say,
Martha, I'm touched by your concern for Mop Boy.
Please don't worry—I assure you—Mop Boy will do
just fine. Where do you think he's from? Brazil? How
about Brazil. Let's say he's managed to get himself
here from Brazil.''

''Why do you say Brazil?'' Tharaud said. ''He's
probably an actor on his day job.''

''You asked what his life was like,'' Cerriere said,
''so I'm telling you what I think, Martha. I think he's
a light-skinned Brazilian. If you don't like Brazil—
how about Lithuania? Hypothetically, of course—
let's say that he's a dark-haired Lithuanian. Or
maybe Honduran. Let's say he's Honduran.''

''He's not Honduran,'' Martha said.

''You think Mop Boy wants to go back to Honduras? Why doesn't Mop Boy want to go back to Honduras? Mop Boy! Mop Boy's not stupid. Something
goes wrong, Mop Boy, obviously, has figured out how

to find someone to take care of him. It was either figuring it out or what? What happens to a mop boy in Honduras? Look at him over there—he's eating an apple Danish! He's drinking cappuccino! The law of Mop Boy—at least, Martha, you can get a hold of it. Mop Boy at least has his mop and pail—at least he knows what and where it is. Mop and pail is mop and pail. Cyberspace, Martha—what can you get a hold of in cyberspace? Have you ever thought of that?''

Cerriere's voice had gotten so loud that the man and woman at the nearby table had gotten up and left. The employees behind the counter kept looking up from their work at him.

Cerriere stood up and put his suit jacket on. Tharaud and I were still sitting. He spread his long hands flat on the table, leaning forward, his voice low, almost a whisper. ''The entire world's banking, communications systems, everything on TV, in books, movies, newspapers, music, everything,'' he said, ''everything that can be is being reduced to digital bits, Martha. Ideas! You like ideas so much, Martha . . .''

He stood straight again, taking his briefcase off the chair. ''How's a terabit for an idea?'' he asked with a smile. ''You don't even know what it is, do you, Martha? It's a new optical fiber—the next generation of optical fibers. Invented by the Japanese. A trillion bits a second—transmitting the equivalent, in one second, of twelve million telephone calls *simultaneously*. And terabits are *before* the next wave of telecommunications mergers and joint ventures starts kicking in. Everything is up for grabs, Martha, and no one even

knows what he—or she, or she, Martha—is grab-
bing."

Cerriere stopped. "Except, for my client," he
said. "My client knew precisely what he was grab-
bing. That you are right about, Martha. About that,
I admit, you are absolutely right."

The Melting Pot

ALEXANDER HAMILTON. HIS GRAVE. RIGHT HERE. The one with the small stone pyramid on top. You can still read the inscription. IN MEMORY OF ALEXANDER HAMILTON. Forty-seven years old when he died—let's see, when did he die? Eighteen-five. The duel with Aaron Burr. Almost two hundred years later and still no one knows what really went down. Hamilton and Burr were, you realize, both lawyers.''

"I forgot Hamilton was a lawyer," I said.

"Only the most successful commercial lawyer of his time," James Shumate said. We were walking on Rector Street beside the spiked iron fence that surrounds Trinity Church Cemetery. "Hamilton was George's—Washington's—boy. No one's fool, either. Founded the Bank of New York, back over here, on Wall Street—still in existence. Founded the Bank of the United States, the Federal Reserve of its day. Founded the *New York Post*, still in existence. They still have his picture at the top of the front page, above the headline, a little cartoon of this man in a wig. Right above—what was that one headline? KHA-DAFY GOES DAFFY, TURNED INTO A TRANSVESTITE DRUGGIE. I wonder if Hamilton—if one of his banks —would have financed Muammar. I wonder how Hamilton would have gotten along with the *Post*'s present-day owner. Do you think Rupert Murdoch thinks of himself as Hamilton's successor-in-interest? My opinion? No comparison. Hamilton had *much* more money than Murdoch—and Murdoch's worth what? How many billions? Not only did Al marry into money, but he made some for himself on the side. Oh, yes," Shumate added, "last, but certainly not least, Al was, of course, a Founding Father of the United States of America. Did you notice who was buried ten feet away from him? Robert Fulton."

"Of the Fulton steamship?" I asked.

"Of Fulton Street, too," said Shumate. "Died eleven years after Hamilton."

We approached the corner of Rector Street and Trinity Place. Shumate and I had known each other for almost fifteen years. We were introduced by a classmate of his from college whom I knew in law school. We both were from the Midwest—I was from Detroit, Shumate from Chicago. We would get to-gether two or three times a year for lunch, usually at India House, an old club located downtown on Han-over Square, which Shumate belonged to. Since it was a warm, summery May day, Shumate suggested that we get take-out and eat outside. Over six feet tall, he walked with his head and shoulders erect, looking straight ahead as he talked. His voice was low and steady. "Got to give Hamilton credit," Shumate continued. "There's Jefferson, down South, deliberating on liberty and justice for all, getting off on his slave girls and how much he hated all dem rich New York and Philadelphia lawyers and bankers who didn't want to do business with him, while Alex is marrying into the wealthiest family in the Empire State, starting up *the* two most powerful banks of his time, cozying up—some say *real* cozy—to his Commander in Chief, becoming, last but not least, *the* first Secretary of the Treasury of these United States. This is, of course, after he convinces his fellow Founding Fathers, most of whom are lawyers, that you need a government run by those who have the cash, or don't bother having a government at all."

Shumate pointed his right index finger at me. "Lifetime appointments to the Supreme Court? Hamilton. Also advocated a lifetime Presidency and lifetime senators and governors appointed by the lifetime President. That one he lost. I guess." Shumate smiled. "You might say he lost that one with Burr, too. A *superlative* lawyer, Al. There were all these shitty low-grade bonds left over from the Articles of Confederation—all this worthless currency floating around—when they moved the government from Philadelphia to just over here on Wall Street, to Federal Hall. Where there's that statue of George now. I love that corner! There's old Federal Hall right across the street from the New York Stock Exchange and the Morgan Bank building. You know about the bomb in the Morgan Bank building, don't you? You don't?

Right after World War I. A bomb in a pushcart. Probably like one of those pushcarts today you can buy a gyro from. Hundreds of people injured, thirty or so dead. Never found out who did it, either. Of course no one in the bank was hurt—just the poor suckers who happened to be walking down the street. Unbeknownst to our peddler-bomber, old J.P. was off in the Highlands tossing down scotches. The damage to the building's still there—they never fixed it.

"So Hamilton, the first Secretary of the Treasury of the United States of America, pays top dollar for all this junk, much of which, after he revalues it, ends up in his banks. No violation of the law. The law was what he—he and his fellow Founding Fathers—said it was. They just clean-slate invented it, the law. Divvied everything up. Hamilton wanted Treasury, George owed him, so"—Shumate laughed—"'Here, Al, with heartfelt appreciation, it's all yours, the Treasury of these United States.'"

We came to the corner of Rector and Trinity Place. Shumate had suggested that we eat at the outdoor plaza at the World Trade Center. We walked, first, south a block on Trinity Place to a take-out restaurant, Sale & Pepe, located on the ground level of a newer building, One Exchange Plaza. We crossed a narrow, one-block-long one-way street, Exchange Alley. "Bet you didn't know there was an Exchange Alley in our metropolis, did you? I walk over here a lot, usually around one-thirty if I can," Shumate said. "From my office, down Exchange Place to Broadway, then over to Rector, down Rector to Trinity Place, Greenwich, Washington Street, West Street— I still think of it as the highway. On nice days I go over to Battery Park City—the promenade, the Japanese gardens down near Battery Park. I sometimes have a late lunch over here at Giovanni's. Mostly I pick something up on the run.''

"Do you ever go into Trinity Church?''

"I have,'' Shumate said. "I like it in the late afternoon—it's very quiet. There's a poor box at the back. A list of announcements. Sermons. On greed. Booze. Losing one's soul. Got to love it—you open the door and there is the Street.''

Shumate glanced at the sky. "Looks like there might be rain,'' he said, "though it seems to be clearing over the river. I love weather like this. That's what I like about it down here in the boondocks, with all us boons. You can walk.''

At Sale & Pepe there was a long take-out line. "Did I ever tell you,'' Shumate asked as we waited, "about—late last September, early October—when I was walking in Battery Park? I don't think I have. It was one of those Indian-summer afternoons—you know, when the light's so bright it blasts your head off. Staten Island was covered—you could hardly see it. It was this silver-green and blue haze. One of those days it feels like you're on the Mediterranean down here. Anyway, I was walking in the Park when I came to these large tents on the promenade, near the old Marine Fire Department building. I thought, at first, I was on a movie set. I asked a security guard, 'Why the tents?' He said it was a private party. Someone had rented Battery Park! This is two football fields away from the new Holocaust Memorial they were building—a block or so farther away from where, each spring, there's the Cirque du Soleil. Maybe I'm just getting old—I told Caryn, I said, you know, it's all a farce. The whole thing is a farce."

"You remember, don't you," I asked, "what farce means in Latin?"

"Of course I remember. To stuff. Like stuffing a goose. Which is cool. Goose stuffing. I like goose. Caryn disagrees with me. She says it's a bazaar. One big carnival freak-show bazaar."

"A vanity fair," I said.

"We're *waaaaaay* past vanity fair, man—way past. Too far past—if you want to know the truth—for my sensitive soul. But, then, what do I know? I —I don't know nuthin'."

Shumate recommended the albacore-tuna sandwich, which we both ordered. He also ordered two small bottles of Pellegrino for himself. "So," he said as we waited, "you want to know what I think about lawyers. What a lawyer thinks about the law. And you've come to me for the zebra perspective, right?"

"Zebra?"

"I iz da—what's the word these days? You know, I got black and white stripes, man. Wha' we'z call'd deez days—*zeeeee*bras!"

Shumate laughed. "My son," he said, "my eldest. Comes home the other day—he's talking about Caucasoids. Caucasoids! So I say to him, 'Son, if white folk are Caucasoids, what does that make us, Negroids? What does that make your Asian sisters and bro's at your school, Mongoloids?' Now, this ain't no dumb boy. Best schools, high test scores, studies hard, good grades—and, I am proud to say, high-aptitude street-smarts. Good kid. Manages to manage his mother and me—I must acknowledge—quite adeptly. Seventeen years old, already taller than I am—I think he's gonna hit six-two, six-three. He's got more melanin in him than I do—he's dark, very dark, like my mother. So do you know what he says to me? He gives me this 'Dad, you-are-a-fuckin'-zebra' look. He says, 'Dad'—he repeats 'Dad' to make sure I get it—'we are African-Americans.' Well, yes, son, I was going to say, I am aware of that. But me? I don't say nuthin'. I go instead to my source. One of these taxi drivers from the islands. Hamilton, incidentally, was from the islands. Nevis. My man, he's Haitian. I ask him, 'What should we be calling ourselves these days, brother?' He looks at me through his rearview mirror, sees the way I'm dressed, the briefcase, smells the cologne, and gives me a 'I ain't your brother, brother' look, then, in perfect French—a language whose pronunciation I've never been able to perfect—says, 'Negre.' " Shumate laughed again. "Negre! So I am negre. So you want my negre answer, right?"

I said that I'd told someone who wasn't a lawyer that I wanted to talk to a black lawyer about what it was like being a lawyer, and that he asked me why—why should it make any difference?

"What do you mean—difference?" asked Shumate.

"Whether it makes any difference that a lawyer is black or not."

"Was this person Caucasoid?"

"Yes."

"Well," Shumate said, "he may have had a point."

Our sandwiches were ready. We paid and walked

out on Trinity Place, then turned toward the World Trade Center, walking alongside the long, high copper-colored Trinity Church wall. Shumate took a deep breath. "Man, that spring air feels good." He stopped. "You really are"—there was a smile on his face—"going to make me answer this, aren't you? On this nice spring day you're going to make me talk about what I think it's like to be a negre lawyer. Very well, then," he said with a sigh. "The negre lawyer. I should, I suppose, put my biases up front. I happen to be among those who still think slavery—that particular brand of American slavery—definitely has something to do with it."

We came to Liberty Street. "Right up here," Shumate said, pointing at the World Trade Center across the street, "is the busiest place in downtown Manhattan. Six, seven thousand people an hour pass by here at this time every weekday." We crossed Liberty, walking on Church Street toward the Trade Center. "You know," Shumate continued, his voice reflective, "I can remember when I was a kid, hearing one of my uncles saying the foreman in the foundry he worked in kept a red-hot poker stuck up his ass from the time he punched in to the time he punched out, and my other uncle—my uncle who was involved in the union—commenting, 'Well, why are you surprised? They used to stick red-hot pokers up our forefathers' asses, and you know what they stuck up our foremamas' asses.' He'd say slaves were 'employees of a sort.' He used to talk like that. Slaves were 'employees of a sort.' "

"This was your uncle the steelworker?"

"I had two uncles who were steelworkers. This is

my uncle who was a union steward. 'It's not like you had a lot of freedom to contract your labor, now, did you?'—that's the kind of thing he used to say. When I was in law school he'd say, 'But, of course, whether you can, and under which conditions you can, sell your labor—of course that would have nothing to do with law, now, would it?' He'd look me right in the eye and tell me, 'Your great-grandparents, remember, were slaves.' 'United States of America slaves,' is how he put it. Well, he was right. Nothing''—Shumate shrugged—''I can do about it. It's not like I'm making it up. You take away all the 'that was a hundred years ago,' 'that was then, this is now,' the 'my grandparents came here with nothing, either'—you take all that horseshit away, and what you've got is a fact. The fact that my father and mother's grandparents . . .''

Shumate paused. ''You know, don't you, that there's no mention of race in the Constitution? My uncle pointed that out to me. No one in law school ever did. The original Constitution of the United States refers to 'free Persons' and 'all other Persons,' i.e., *slaves*. It was about *slaves—slave* labor.''

We turned onto a wide sidewalk promenade and walked awhile again in silence. ''You know, every once in a while . . .'' Shumate said, stopping again. ''Every once in a while it, like, comes to the forefront and slaps you across the side of your head. The fact that my slave great-granddaddies and great-grandmamas weren't citizens until ninety years after the declaration of life, liberty and the pursuit of happiness—now, that's had no effect at all on the way our laws are made today, has it? How could that be?

No way that could be! It happened so long ago! All dem negres blessed with citizenship—one hundred and thirty years ago now. What's their problem? After the most brutal, sadistic war in the history of the world up until that time, our new former-slave negre citizens could—just like all of dem free white males —simply go right into the free market and sell their labor, now, couldn't they? The classical theory of contract! You walk into the Bank of New York and borrow a little bit of money with yo' water pail as yo' co-lat-a-ral, start up a little chitlin's business right over here on Water Street, right?"

We continued walking. Ahead of us was a farmer's market. Across the street was the Millenium Hotel, with its fifty-five-story black glass façade.

"How's your father doing?" Shumate asked.

"He's all right," I said. "He's had a series of small strokes. There nothing that can be done about it. He can walk, which is good. And he's very clear —he can talk. That whole generation's getting old. How's your mom doing?"

"Not bad. We got her living up in Evanston."

"How old is she now?"

"Pushing eighty. Still sharp. Still ornery, too."

"Is your uncle still alive?"

"No, he passed two years ago."

"I remember that now. I'm sorry."

"I think of him every day. You don't realize it at the time, but there he was, a union steward, and reading all the time. All the time teaching me, too. I remember watching those old *Amos 'n' Andy* TV shows, there was a lawyer character, his name, I remember, was Algonquin J. Calhoun. Algonquin J. Calhoun!

When I was growing up I remember two lawyers who lived in the neighborhood—I have no idea what they did. Wills? Who had a will? Real estate? Only if you worked as a front man for the white real estate block busters—remember those slime? My uncle would have made a *great* lawyer. He was the one who made sure my brother and I went to Saint Ignatius. He was the one who told me to study Greek. He didn't give a shit about God—he cared about protecting our minds. Who he worshipped was Dinah Washington. I think he had a thing with her once. When she died, he got a bad case of the blues. He never married, my uncle —no kids. Can you imagine, a black man, his generation, never married, no sissy, no kids?''

Shumate's face broke into a smile. ''You know who I thought of the other day? Gilroy.''

''Gilroy?'' I said. ''What's Gilroy up to?''

''I always forget that you know him. How do you know him, again?''

''I don't want to get into that,'' I said. ''Is he still at Caldwell?''

''Barely. Your standard worried-about-getting-let-go Caldwell partner. The ass-kissing doesn't work for a Gilroy the way it used to. Now, there was a man who could lip-suction! I was such a better lawyer than Gilroy. I have to give him credit, though—he certainly effectively used my black ass.''

''What kind of things are you doing these days?''

''Bonds. Financing. Municipal bonds.''

''How's business?''

''Good. We're, like, the premier municipal-bond firm in the country, you know. I'm always busy. Things are good.''

"What's it mean to do municipal bonds?"

"What do you mean, what's it mean?"

"Who are your clients?"

"Banks. Underwriters. We represent everybody. Municipalities."

"Where do the banks come in?"

"We do a lot of L-C's."

"L-C's?"

"My cousin, Lucien Cameron Shumate—L. C. Shumate. Golden Gloves heavyweight medal winner, the country of Chicago, nineteen-hundred and sixty-five. What do you think I mean?"

"The country of Chicago?"

"That's how we Chi-*cahg*-o-ins—notice the correct pronunciation—refer to it. The country of Chicago. What's that country in South America? You know, the small one? Bolivia! Are you going to tell me Bolivia's a country and Chicago's not?"

"Your cousin won the Chicago Golden Gloves?"

"Nineteen sixty-five. One mean mother, too."

"Did he go on?"

"Quit. Got knocked out in the nationals by a huge kid—from, of all places, Memphis. LeRoy something or other—he changed his name to LeRoi. The French touch, you know. The brothers called him Elvis. Lucien's a court officer in San Francisco. He used to say if a LeRoy from Memphis nicknamed Elvis could punch his lights out, then what could a Sonny Liston do?"

"What's an L-C?"

"A letter of credit. You know, from a bank? Default—remember? If the issuer defaults, the bond-holders draw on the letter of credit. The bank can then—for what it's worth—sue the issuer. It's fairly mechanical—which I don't mind. It's all right with me. I've also been doing some mortgage securitization."

"What's a mortgage securitization?"

"I'm not sure I know what it is," Shumate said with a laugh. "You make mortgages into securities. There are all these new finance techniques. Lawyer creations. A mortgage securitization is when a bank purchases mortgage portfolios, then places them in trusts, or in newly created corporations. You use the trust or the new corporation to issue new securities—mortgage pass-through certificates is what they're technically called. The debt payments to the mortgage holders are paid with the cash flow from the mortgage portfolios. The client—it gets a little more complicated here. Basically, the client gets the difference between the payments it receives from the individual mortgages and the coupon it pays on the pass-through securities. Me, I think—well, everything depends on the money coming in on the mortgages. The economy starts to drop—if the mortgages aren't paid, et cetera, et cetera. But that"—Shumate shrugged—"ain't my problem. When it happens, we'll do what we did when all the junk from the eighties went bad—we'll just shift over into bankruptcy.

"We used to do," he said, "radio-station deals before the law changed. Did you follow any of that?"

I said I hadn't.

"You didn't read about this in the papers? A couple of years ago. It was a big political deal. If you owned a radio station and you sold it to buyers with at least a twenty-percent minority—God, how I hate that word—a twenty-percent minority interest, you, the seller, could defer capital gains. There was a federal statute. What it meant, of course, is that the mostly *non*-minority buyers would get a good deal— you could get the seller to knock off part of what he'd gain from his capital gains from the purchase price. Someone, though, in the press got into it—affirmative action, a boondoggle for the niggers, et cetera, et cetera. They repealed it. A partner of mine did a number of them—they always liked to have a black face at the table. One of our clients was a very prominent African-American. From a very old and distinguished Washington, D.C., family. Groton and Amherst. The Yale Law School. The Carter Administration. A multimultimillionaire. Hangs with stars of television, screen, and court. Including the basketball court— he's part owner of one of the teams, I can't remember which one. He's the twenty-percent minority interest in a deal to purchase a radio station in Georgia. The guy selling the station is a Lee Atwater–white-Negro-cooning type who loves to wax eloquent about how much he loves Percy Sledge. At the closing he starts singing, falsetto, 'When a Man Loves a Woman.' He says to our man—our man, mind you, dines with *royalty*—Lee asks him, 'Are you all gonna make my radio station into rhythm and blues?'

"Can you believe it? My partner—he can't control himself. Goes and violates Negro Lawyer Rule Number One—he couldn't resist. 'No,' he says to Lee, 'no, sir. Funk. We are going to format your station *funk*. Funkentelechy.' "

"Funkentelechy?"

"Yeah, man. Funkentelechy. The Parliament–Funkadelic record from the late seventies—*Funkentelechy vs. the Placebo Syndrome*. Though, I must admit, my favorite Clinton—George, not William Jefferson—has always been 'I Wanna Testify,' when no one knew who George was—before P-Funk—when he was lead singer for the Parliaments. The Parliaments! George always was a believer in the rule of law! I'm sure the song had a subliminal influence on my becoming a lawyer. You don't know what funkentelechy is? Funk—dash—entelechy?"

"Entelechy's a philosophical term, isn't it? I've always had trouble pronouncing it."

"Funk-enta-le-kee," Shumate said. "Entelechy—it's the vital principle. The soul as opposed to the body. George is from your hometown, man. You don't think he knows entelechy when he sees it?"

"What's Negro Lawyer Rule Number One?" I asked.

Shumate looked at me and smiled. "This is a secret, man. You're not going to go telling everybody, now, are you? Negro Lawyer Rule Number One? Well," he said, "let me put it this way. I will simply put it this way. Me? I cannot afford to go into fits. Or temper tantrums. Not do my hair right. Dress like a slob. Cultivate the madman aura. Shit! What do you think happens if you start acting like a crazy nigger? So. Negro Lawyer Rule Number One is act like a smart nigger. The most dangerous thing in the world—at least in this world —is a smart negre. Man, woman, child—no one quite ever knows what might be going through a smart negre's mind.''

Shumate and I found a place to eat on a stone bench close to a huge bronze sculpture of the Earth, a fountain of water encircling its base. We were surrounded by the World Trade Center's towers. Because of the constant rushing sound of water from the fountain, we had to speak louder than we had been. Shumate twisted open a small bottle of Pellegrino, poured it into a plastic cup, then took a sip. ''You know,'' he said, ''back in the eighties, after I left Caldwell, around the time all the leveraging began coming apart, my uncle—he was around seventy then—sends me James Baldwin's last book, *The Evidence of Things Not Seen*, with a note, which I still have. I keep it as a bookmark. 'You're a lawyer,' it says, 'read this.' I know you don't know the book— nobody does. It's Baldwin on the children missing and murdered in Atlanta back in the early eighties— Wayne Williams, remember? The title is taken from Saint Paul. 'Faith is the substance of things hoped for, the evidence of things not seen.' That's one of the epigraphs—the other is from William Blake. 'A dog starv'd at his master's gate predicts the ruin of the state.' Baldwin did *not* mess around!

''You know, I never really thought about it back then. You take things so much for granted. How much my uncle read. There he was, a steelworker for U.S. Steel. The South Works. He used to laugh at my brother and me, when we'd be reading Caesar, he'd say shit like, 'You come down to where I work and

I'll show you some Caesar.' He actually got us jobs during the summers—in the foundry—not easy to pull off at the time if you were of our color. I still remember what we made—that glorious summer of sixty-six. Two dollars and sixty-two cents an hour.''

We started eating our sandwiches. Shumate looked around the plaza and up at the two Trade Center towers. "No one," he went on, "was smarter than Jimmy Baldwin. *There* was a genius. Gay—but did anyone give a shit? He was *blessed.* He'd get up, when he was a child, before the congregation and preach— he was blessed. No matter what you want to say about black folk, they have a reverential respect—a holy respect—for those who are blessed. My uncle used to read everything by Baldwin. He'd take notes. Baldwin and Gibbon. And Oswald Spengler—of all people, he'd be quoting Oswald Spengler! He used to write down quotations on pieces of paper and carry them around in his pockets—he wore those green cotton denim work pants workers used to wear back then, you know, the kind you'd buy from Monkey Ward's or from Sears—and he'd read them to you. Anyhow, here's one for you. Compliments of Zebra. Pretty much verbatim. 'In any case'—that is Baldwin's lead-in—'in any case . . .' ''

Shumate took another bite of his sandwich and finished his bottle of water. He then opened the second bottle that he'd bought. " 'In any case,' " he continued, " 'in any case this country's not so much a vicious racial cauldron'—Jimmy says—'because many, if not most countries, are that. It's not so much a vicious racial cauldron as a paranoid color wheel.' That's what he says. Paranoid color wheel! 'Some people would like to step out of their White'—capital W—'skins and some people loathe their Black'—capital B—'skins.' Some people hate and fear their white kinfolk, others hate and fear their black kinfolk. And''—Shumate paused—''I want to get this right. 'However we confront or fail to confront this most crucial truth concerning our history, American history, everybody pays for it and everybody knows it.' Whoever murdered these children could have been *anyone, anyone,* he says—cop, teacher, bus driver, next-door neighbor—anyone of any color. All would, or could, have had a motive—or the same motive. A paranoid color wheel! Man, I find that incredible. Not one to mince his words, not Jimmy! I quote again. Quote. 'Underlying the tremendous unwillingness to believe that a black person could be murdering black children was the specifically Southern'—capital S— 'the specifically Southern knowledge and experience of how much black blood's in white veins, and how much white blood's in black veins.'

''Now, wha' do dat ha' ta do wit' da law, huh? When anyone of any color could, or would, have had a motive to commit a crime against anyone of any color. What's that have to do with the law? Man, it is it exactly. It is exactly it! It's like what my uncle said during the Tawana Brawley thing—it was right before he passed—remember that? My uncle said everyone was missing the point. Paranoid color wheel, he'd say. The logic, he said, of your law and of your civilization. 'Take it from an old Negro steelworker from the South Side of Chicago—that's your civilization,' he said. 'What could have happened in fact happened.' It didn't happen, but it could have

happened—therefore, it happened. 'Deductive thinking, right?' he said to me. You wonder''—Shumate
asked—''why the law doesn't work right? Farce! It's
more than farce. A farce is what it's supposed to be
—a show, a spectacle. That way, nothing ever gets
really down.''

Shumate stopped again, catching his breath. ''You
know, I was thinking,'' he went on, ''when we were
in college. Do you realize it was one hundred years
after the end of the Civil War to the time we began
college? I was remembering how much my old man
and my uncle used to argue. My old man was a security guard for the *Chicago Tribune*. He was proud
of it, too. He took the El to work every day. He never
wanted any trouble. All my old man wanted was to
be left alone. The defining moment of his life was
when he was in the Army, the Tuskegee Airmen, the
black brigade, or whatever it was they called themselves—he used to tell us war stories. My uncle never
went into the Army. It was never clear why. I think
it was a physical deferment—no one ever talked
about it. My uncle was against Vietnam early on. He'd
get into a rap—man, they'd start cursing—and my
mother, my mother who went to mass every morning
to pray for our souls, she'd start to cry. My uncle
studied the Romans. 'Slaves, goddamn slave states!'
he used to shout. 'Make people into meat for animals.
That's what they're doing to our children in this war,'
he said. 'They're making them into nothing.' He used
to get pissed off at what he called all this 'mau-mau-
mo-mo-fo-fo-shit.' Commodification—I shit you not—
was the word he used. He used to say it's black boys
fighting the goddamn war. 'No different than slaves,

like Roman slaves,' he said, 'and they're coming back home drug addicts, they're coming home knowing how to kill, they're coming home crazy.' I remember he'd open his eyes wide and repeat, a few inches away from my father's face, he'd, like, almost spit the word into my old man's face—'crazy!' He used to, my uncle, use the word nigger all the time—nigger-this, nigger-that. One time he overdid it and my old man lost it. I thought they were going to get into a fistfight. You know what my uncle used to do?''

Shumate finished his sandwich and water, putting the empty cup, bottles, wrapping, and napkins back into the paper bag. ''Remember when Ali claimed he was a conscientious objector? His case went, remember, all the way to the Supreme Court? He won, too. My uncle used to take the El down to Hyde Park, he'd go to the University of Chicago Law School library after work and photocopy—it used to cost like a quarter a page, remember?—everything he could find on the case. When I was in law school he used to argue with me about the distinction between law and fact—he knew more about administrative law than my very famous professor did. Here I was learning legal realism at the law school where it began—Roscoe Pound—and my uncle would be writing me letters about the Ali case, saying that the problem the legal system had was that a Negro who changed his name to Muhammad, who happened also to be the heavyweight champion of the world, could never have any kind of *conscience*. 'They're trying to make him into a fact,' he said—can you believe it? That's the kind of thing he used to say. 'They're trying to make him into a fact.' ''

We sat in silence a few minutes and then started walking back to Church Street. Shumate tossed our trash into a bin and then stopped a moment to look at a rock-hewn pyramid-shaped sculpture. "Let's walk back on Washington Street," he said when we were on Church Street again. "I've got one more quotation for you," he continued. "One of my uncle's favorites. Spengler. My uncle liked Oswald Spengler. *The Decline*—he'd purposely pronounce it the '*dee-*cline'—*of the West*. This is it."

"You've memorized it?"

"You know, man, the Afro-American oral tradition. Let me get this right now. Oswald Spengler. 'What is described as civilization, then, is the stage of culture at which tradition and personality have lost their immediate effectiveness and every idea'—here's where my uncle would pause—'every idea, to be actualized, has to be put in terms of money.' My uncle used to quote this, and then he'd say that he worked in a steel mill for over thirty years, and that Oswald Spengler was right. Every idea, my uncle would say —including freedom—to be actualized ends up put in terms of money. He loved to say the word 'actualized.' 'Actual—*ized*,' that's how he'd say it—'actual-*ized*.' Then he'd grin. He liked to rile me, too—just enough to make me uneasy. 'Shit,' he'd say, 'black, white, white, black—in the history of the world, what are we talking about, your Afro—your American African Negro? Five, ten, fifteen, twenty million descendants of slaves—it's nothing. Nothing! 'What if,' he'd say, 'what if the truth really is that your civilization, that your law, lawyer, really is an idea that becomes actualized—becomes real—only in terms of money?

Then what?' he'd ask—I can still see him shaking his head. 'Doctors,' he'd say, 'at least doctors got to smell people—touch them. See, smell, touch their pus and their shit. Ever notice'—this was one of his favorites—'ain't no doctor politicians?' 'Lawyers,' he'd say, 'what do lawyers feel? Tell me, what do they feel?' Then he'd start to laugh. I thought of my uncle the other day. One in three African-American men in their twenties is in jail, or on probation, or on parole. One in three! These are kids just a few years older than my son and my daughter. My uncle, I said to myself, would have had a field day with this. Man, you wouldn't have been able to shut him up!''

We'd crossed Liberty and were heading toward Washington Street. "You know," Shumate said, "your people used to have a community right down over here—down here on Washington Street. Little Syria. What is it that you are, again? A Maronite? I've never gotten it exactly straight—what's a Maronite, again?''

"It's one of the Eastern Rites of the Catholic Church," I said. "Named after a one-eyed monk, Saint Maron. He lived in the fourth century, supposedly.''

"Lebanon, right?'' asked Shumate.

"Now it's Lebanon. Then it probably would have been part of the Byzantine Empire.''

"You said 'supposedly'?''

"It's not certain he existed. Like Saint Patrick. When my grandparents came here—right before the First World War—Lebanon was a district of Syria, and Syria was part of the Ottoman Empire.''

"It was right down here,'' Shumate said. "Where

the entrance to Brooklyn–Battery Tunnel now is. Robert Moses wiped it out and everything else around there. He wanted to build another bridge—instead of a tunnel—to Brooklyn. Did you know that?"

"A bridge from here to Brooklyn?"

"Over Battery Park, Governors Island, the East River, into Brooklyn. The blue bloods said no way—they beat him. It was the only time he ever lost."

"Was Robert Moses a lawyer?" I asked.

"Don't think so. Didn't have to be. He was like Boss Tweed—the lawyers and the politicians worked for him. He made some crack once about Roosevelt —who *was* a lawyer. He went to Harvard. Moses said Roosevelt wasn't quite a real man because he was a cripple. Roosevelt hated his guts, but wasn't a whole lot even he could do. You know something else I recently saw? There are now more Muslims in the United States than Episcopalians."

"Do you know any Muslims?" I asked.

"Muslims of the Nation of Islam?" Shumate asked. "Because I have clients who are Muslim. The Nation of Islam? No," he said, "not really. Everyone knows someone who's been part of it or around it, though. Clarence Thomas, you know, was heavy into Malcolm. I have a cousin—L.C.'s brother Billy—who worked for Elijah Muhammad after Malcolm was killed, in the late sixties. He claims he never joined, but, no doubt about it, he hung with them. My dad used to talk about guys in his day, during the thirties, who used to walk around the neighborhood— light-skinned, with 'fros. They used to speak, or claimed they spoke—how would anyone know the difference?—Arabic. They'd be carrying around the

Koran. My dad always thought it was a way to make a living. You founded your own church, your own sect—it was a kind of a hustle. It was a way of passing, people being so desperate at the time.''

''Probably that's what Fard did,'' I said.

''Fard was supposed to have been the prophet, or something like that, if I remember right. I remember thinking Elijah Muhammad made Fard up, but, apparently, he didn't. Fard disappeared—in Detroit. Elijah Muhammad met Fard in Detroit. Another one of your homies. You know, I've always wondered how they—the Syrians . . . Well, I really don't. How they financed themselves.''

''They did what Italians did back then and what Chinese, Koreans, Indians do today,'' I said. ''They borrowed from each other.''

''Which black folk never could do. We needed the state to protect us—the very state that had made us slaves. You wonder why there's paranoia!''

We'd walked to the corner of Rector and Washington. ''Negre lawyers—the law and negre lawyers. Two answers,'' Shumate suddenly said, stopping. ''First. The more you abstract the meaning you give to the appellation African-American lawyer, the easier it is to speak about it. I won't tell you who I got that from. Nor will I tell you where I got answer number two. That when you talk about law in the United States of America you are also, directly or indirectly, talking about African-Americans. Or—to paraphrase my second point—everything in America is, as my dad used to say, everything. Ev-a-ree-thing is ev-a-ree-thing! What the people say!

''So, now that I'm done with that,'' Shumate said.

"It was this past Columbus Day—have I told you about this? Tell me if I have.

"I was with Caryn—a dinner. The Union Square Café. Clients, other lawyers, spouses, a fairly big deal—we'd closed it that Friday, this was Sunday. The clients were still in town, so we had dinner, about fifteen of us. Charlotte Hughes—have you ever come across her? She was representing one of the banks. She's sitting there telling everyone how she sat down with a calculator and figured out how much M and A work she's done the past ten years. 'Twenty billion—give or take a hundred million here or there.'"

"She actually said this?"

"Then there's this client. Seems like a nice enough fellow. Drinking a bit too much vino, though—starts to soul-chat. First he says he loves the fact that bankers rule the world. 'They're a helluva lot better than the politicians!' he says, loud, sloppy drunk, big white teeth, you know, ha-ha-ha. Maybe he was overly excited about being in the Big Town, I don't know—he's a client, he can say what he wants. But then he turns serious. Major mood shift. He asks if we know Jesus. You should have seen the look on Charlotte Hughes's face! Let me say," Shumate added in a serious tone, "this kind of question I do not take lightly. I have people in my family who have walked and talked with Jesus. And this is a client—so I'm cool. Except White Tooth won't give it up. He says he's been thinking a whole lot about Jesus, heaven—the Last Judgment. He says he knows for a fact that heaven's an actual place, shaped like a cube, one thousand miles on each side."

Shumate shook his head. "Man, like, what you've

got to do, right? So. We get out of there. It's past midnight—chilly, clear, a beautiful night. People on the street. We decide to walk home—we're over in the Twenties, when we see a mob—I mean this mob! —running down the street at us. It was in the paper the next day. A club—someone opened fire. There were all these kids wounded. A club located in the Martha Washington Hotel."

"The Martha Washington Hotel?"

"The Martha Washington Hotel. A Columbus Day dance in the Martha Washington Hotel. The club's name—the Melting Pot."

"The Melting Pot?"

"The Melting Pot. I shit you not—the Melting Pot!"

Ta Tung

THOSE WHO GET WHERE THEY ARE BY SUCKING OFF anything and anybody. The hacks. And there are those," Charles Morand said, "who get where they are on their merits. That's about it."

"Can't argue with that," Stephen Bell replied, waving his hand to attract the waitress's attention. He ordered a second glass of iced mint tea. We were sitting outdoors at the Café Fledermaus in the South Street Seaport. It was five-thirty, a June afternoon— a strong, warm wind was gusting, strips of bright white clouds tinged pink moving across a luminous, deep blue sky. A small band was playing jazz. An associate of Morand's—a former student of mine— introduced us once before. I'd never met Bell. Bell and Morand knew each other from the late sixties, when they worked for the Department of Housing and

Urban Development's New York City office. Bell was downtown that afternoon for a meeting. Slouched in his chair, his large hands folded in his lap, he was soft-spoken and amiable, with an immediately apparent alertness, his sandy-colored hair half gray, his body small and very thin. After he left H.U.D., he said, he practiced with a number of firms, developing a specialty in bankruptcy. He was a partner now at a one-hundred-fifty-lawyer firm on Park Avenue in the upper Thirties, where he did "everything—corporate, real estate, even some litigation. A few months ago I even litigated an arbitration for a bank client I've done bankruptcy for." Morand went from H.U.D. to the Social Security Administration, where he worked for over a decade. In the late seventies he started his own firm, which now had five lawyers. Thickset and of medium height, with a full head of brown hair—a few strands of gray running through it on the sides—he fixed his light gray eyes on you with an attentive, critical intensity. "Social Security disability, insurance claims, some workers' comp, Medicaid estate planning—I'm doing more and more work with the very old," he said after I asked him about his practice. "Then there's the usual rag bag —I was in Housing Court a week ago. I hadn't been there in years." "You were in Housing Court?" Bell asked incredulously. "Brooklyn Housing Court," Morand said. "Talk about depressing. Nothing worked—the toilets, the water fountains. Plaster peeling from the walls and the ceilings. Almost all women—babies crying. No one—well, hardly no one—speaking English. Now *that*—interpreters—is a growing business. Have to hire them all the time. I asked this one man what language he was interpreting—Punjabi. The courtrooms—they weren't really courtrooms. More like converted offices. The judges function like social workers."

Morand was drinking a vodka on ice, which he finished. "You look tired," Bell said to him. "I am tired," Morand said. "I have a client I want to get on disability who's diabetic—his blood pressure's bad, he has problems with his feet, circulation problems, but the fact that you're diabetic is not enough to get disability. I talk to him. I hear the whole story. Fired from his job, divorced, kids, a son studying criminology at John Jay, a daughter who's left the area—she's married to a computer technician in Omaha, where he's never been invited to visit. His father was an alcoholic, used to beat him up, beat his mother up. A fleeting reference to a stay in a psycho ward. I'm trying to work toward something on the mental side."

"These are paying clients?" Bell asked, laughing.

"Big money," said Morand. "We're so damn busy—I probably need two more people, but I don't want to take them on and then have to let them go. So I end up doing this kind of crap. With what's happening with welfare, I think the amount of work's only going to go up." He moved his chair closer to the table to make room for the waitress to get by. He waited until she'd served the other table, then ordered another vodka, "on ice," he reminded her. "After I'm finished trying to absorb the mental state of my diabetic client," he went on, sucking an ice cube, "*my* daughter calls. Her husband left her and my two grandchildren, and she's being threatened by

her husband's lawyer. I want to kill the fucker. I'm
already drafting a grievance in my mind when I get a
call from the son of a man—not that old, early
seventies—with fairly advanced Parkinson's disease.
The son's a lawyer, a nice enough guy, who doesn't
know the first thing about a trust—he doesn't even
have a will himself. I'm setting up a trust for him. If
we don't protect the father's money, it'll end up going
to a nursing home, because if you have Parkinson's
disease, you eventually suffer dementia—the same
symptoms as Alzheimer's—and if you've got Alzheimer's, you end up in a nursing home. Medicare only
covers, like, nothing—a couple of months—so you
need Medicaid, but to qualify for Medicaid you have
to be poor, but the law is very strict on the transfer
of assets. The son breaks down on the phone. He just
had a kid, he's buying a new home out on Long Island. There's no money in the family—his father was
a New York City junior high school teacher. The old
man hardly knows who he is anymore. Then there's
an older sister who's retarded, living with the father.
She's been the victim of a five-hundred-dollar extor-
tion by a couple in the neighborhood. Well, these
kinds of trusts are not that easy to do within the con-
fines of the statute—considering they change the goddamn thing during every election year—but we do it.
I bill the son, who—I wait a few months—doesn't
send me what he owes me, so I have to write him a
letter, which takes time, of course, and he sends me
the money with a letter of apology. He's got a client
who's in trouble with the I.R.S., which he starts telling me about in his letter.''

"He writes you about a case he has with the I.R.S.?" asked Bell.

"I think he word-processed the facts from his brief into the letter. Three single-spaced pages. The I.R.S. claims his client hasn't been paying F.I.C.A. on fifteen or so employees—the client claims the employees are independent contractors, not employees. I happen to know something about the problem—I think he's playing me for free advice. I'll tell you, it tires me out. I'm getting too old for this shit."

"Ah, you love it," said Bell, taking a sip of his iced mint tea, holding onto his napkin to prevent it from blowing away.

"Yeah, I love it all right," Morand said, raising his glass in a mock toast.

I asked both of them what it had been like at H.U.D.

"Neither of us was there very long—only a couple of years," Bell said. "I was gone by sixty-eight. When did you split?" he asked Morand.

"End of sixty-eight. After Nixon was elected."

"We were there right after it was created," Bell said. "You have to remember the law firms were much, much smaller back then. Government work had prestige—there were a couple of years there when it didn't pay a whole lot less than the top firms were paying. What was it like? I remember doing a lot of work with regs—figuring out what they were doing in Washington. It was really government contracts, is what it was. Can't say I learned a whole lot—other than negatively. I learned not to go near the construction business. I haven't since."

"It was hip at the time," said Morand. "The Peace Corps, the Anti-Poverty program—places like that. They weren't easy jobs to get."

"There was this one guy we knew," said Bell. "Theodore 'Teddy' Lipscomb."

"Listen to this," Morand said.

"Wouldn't you say Teddy was slumming?" Bell asked Morand.

"Lipscomb was a Rhodes Scholar," said Morand. "Where'd he go to law school, again?" he asked Bell.

"Harvard, I think."

"Ate and drank like a pig," said Morand. "Must have learned it in England. Put his mouth right down to his plate, then shoveled it in with both knife and fork. He'd scarf a glass of wine in one gulp. A snifter of cognac"—Morand put his head back and opened his mouth as wide as he could—"bam! Right down the hatch! With a snifter! Then he'd smack his lips and smile. Like this," Morand said, contorting his face into a grin.

"Teddy didn't care," Bell said. "His grandfather—I think it was his grandfather—was the first person in history to put cat food in cans." Bell looked at Morand. "Do you remember what you said when he asked you what your sport was?"

"Fucking," Morand said. "I told him it was fucking. Teddy got the biggest kick out of that."

"One of the greatest statements I've ever heard was Lipscomb's," Bell said. "He announced to us one morning—we were on the subway up to Harlem—that his only rule of thumb was not to stick his tongue into any orifice he couldn't put his thumb into. He was serious, too."

"Lipscomb wasn't stupid," Morand said.

"He was an idiot," said Bell.

I asked what he did now. "Vice President and head counsel for Kassel," Morand said. "I saw him a couple of months ago at that Indian restaurant on Fifty-eighth Street—I always forget the name."

"Dawat," said Bell. "I like that place."

"Dawat," Morand repeated. "That's where it was. He was having lunch with a table of Japanese. He waved to me with that little half-assed kind of gesture of the hand, like a weak beat-off."

"You know who I ran into?" Bell said. "Munson."

"Munson? Really? Where'd you run into Munson? Munson," Morand turned to me and said, "is really —I mean really—smart. He was an Assistant U.S. Attorney when we worked at H.U.D. We worked on this one—it must have been the first H.U.D. fraud case—with him. He's a very powerful partner at Broderick & Williams. Does huge—central-bank level—debt-restructuring deals. International securities, financing—big stuff. Decent guy. Absolutely first-rate. Wasn't he an Assistant Secretary of Commerce, or Treasury, or something like that?"

"I'm not sure. I think it was Treasury. Under Reagan," said Bell.

"Where'd you see Munson?" asked Morand.

"At the Hotel Intercontinental. I was there for something or other when, out of nowhere, there he was walking toward me by himself, head down, this terrible look on his face. He was walking right past me, so I said, 'Robert, Robert.' "

"Did he recognize you?" Morand asked.

"I think so," said Bell. "I reminded him who I was. He seemed to be in a kind of trance. He shook my hand—he was cordial. I asked him if everything was all right. He said, 'No. No. Everything is not all right,' then continued on his way."

"He said he wasn't all right?" Morand shook his head. "That is fucking eerie."

There was a long silence. Morand sat back in his chair, holding his glass in his lap. "So," he said to me, "who is this you're meeting here?"

"A college roommate of a cousin," I said. "She's a sixth-year associate at Daley Pincus."

There was silence again. Bell ordered another iced tea and asked Morand if, when he left, he was going uptown. Morand said he was. Bell said he'd leave with him, that they could share a taxi.

Bell looked around. "It's nice down here," he said. He asked Morand if he came to the Seaport often.

"I like it in summer," he said. "After work."

"Are you still in the Woolworth Building?" Bell asked.

"The same place," said Morand.

Bell asked me if I'd ever seen the view from Morand's office. I said I hadn't. "He's up near the top. It faces south and west. You can see the ocean."

"This place can be a scene," said Morand. "A week ago I was here and a woman—clearly in a psychosis—walks up with nothing else on except a filthy pair of jeans."

"Did you ask her"—Bell smiled—"if she needed a lawyer?"

"She had nothing else on," Morand said. "She

was bare-breasted. No shoes. There were a couple of tables of low-grade—I don't know what they were. Russians, maybe. I'm not sure. Big. Mean-looking, too. Then there were the tourists. Germans. They see Café Fledermaus—Fledermaus, I don't know if you know, in German it means bat. As you can see, it's a nice place—they think it's just like at home. Except for this woman—whom they look at in horror, like she's walked right out of hell. No one knows what to do. The Russians and the Americans ignore her—a couple of them start making fun of her. The young girl who's the hostess tonight—over there," Morand said, nodding his head—"she's part Asian, part black. From Trinidad. A year out of an all-girls Catholic school in Port-au-Prince."

"How do you know that?" asked Bell.

"I asked her," Morand said. "The woman came up to her—the girl was terrified. She started freaking out."

"What'd you do?" Bell asked.

"Watched. Once I realized I wasn't going to get physically hurt. The rent-a-cops came and ushered her out of the Seaport. She went wandering up Fulton and disappeared—into the madding crowd."

Bell finished his iced tea and turned to me. "What you asked earlier," he said. "If I thought the practice of law had changed. What I wanted to say was, the deals are more complicated than they used to be. The world is more complicated. Business is more complicated. That's the biggest difference. What twenty years ago was a complex deal is simple—elementary school—today. The simplest deals today are harder than the hardest deals were fifteen, twenty years ago.

The young people coming into the business—they just
don't know very much. How can they? It takes so
goddamn long to train them, too."

"We didn't know very much, either," Morand
said. "They're no more and no less stupid than we
were."

"I didn't say they were stupid," said Bell. "I said
that the problem is that it takes too much time to
teach them. You said it yourself—you don't want to
hire them and take the time and money to teach them
and then have to let them go. What's really happened
is that those we do hire are billing four to five hundred hours a year more, on average, than ten years
ago. The other thing is—because everything is more
complicated—you end up doing it yourself. You also
end up doing it yourself because you need the bill-
ables. I'm billing two hundred hours a year more on
average than I did ten years ago. Limited partner-
ships, the tax side, dissolution, winding up, the kinds
of bankruptcies you see—none of it's gotten any easier, and it never was easy. You forget how long it
takes to get the basics down, but now it takes longer,
and the basics keep changing. There's also a lot more
guile."

Bell paused. He shifted forward in his chair. "I
don't remember having to watch myself all the time,
the way I have to now. Take documents, for example.
You've got lawyers telling clients to destroy documents—they implicate their clients in the fraud.
There are clients who want their lawyers to commit
fraud, so the lawyers are in it with them. Billing. It's
worse than ever. Maybe I shouldn't say worse." He

rubbed the back of his neck. "Let's just say it hasn't gotten any better."

"It's always been a problem," said Morand. "Why should it be any less a problem when there's more pressure to bill?"

"In the eighties, there'd be guys who'd bill whole days when they were out fucking call girls," Bell said. "Everyone knew it, no one cared, there was so much money flying around. I was talking the other day to a partner I know at Simon Skidmore. They hired a partner laterally from Podell Phelps & Orten, whom my friend doesn't care for—never has. He tells me— he's telling me this—the guy is overbilling, deluxe. If you're overbilling at Podell Phelps, by definition it's deluxe. Those guys get hundred-thousand-dollars-a-year bonuses. Everyone—he's telling me this—knows it, too. No one knows what to do about it. There are a lot of people out there on the edge of criminality. A lot of real desperadoes."

"Guile!" Morand said. "It's fraud. Pure and simple fraud. As well as a patent violation of the Code of Professional Responsibility. Remember the Code of Professional Responsibility? It's not only a violation of the Code if you commit fraud, but also if you have knowledge of a lawyer committing it—if you see it and you don't do anything about it, you're violating the Code."

"A rule honored in the breach," said Bell.

"So what do you do about it, Stephen?" Morand asked.

"What do you mean, what do I do about it? I use it to my advantage, is what I do. I'm clean—I'm not stealing from anyone. Everyone gets real nervous when you bring it up. So every once in a while you bring it up. You let them know you know what's going on. They start twitching. Their eyes start shifting back and forth. You'd be surprised the bargaining advantage it can give you."

"It's you guys who've caused it," said Morand.

"What do you mean, you guys?" asked Bell.

"Everyone's got to have the cash," Morand replied. "Desperadoes! Like a partner at Podell Phelps is desperate! The whole goddamn show is so fucking leveraged. From top to bottom. Everyone's got to have their Mercedes, summer homes."

"You've got a summer home," said Bell.

"All right," Morand said, "you're right. I, too, have a summer home. I drive a BMW, too. You're right, Stephen. I make money the same way you make money."

"Fuck you," said Bell. "What you do isn't a whole lot different from what I do."

"I have very different clients than you do, Stephen."

"So what? You're not your clients. You're not them. What's the difference? My clients are victims, too. They have grievances, they have rights. They're people. I help them. I get paid for it. They're happy when I solve their problems."

"The difference is that the poor . . ." Morand stopped.

"I know what you want to say," Bell said. "The poor get fucked by the system. The reason you're having trouble saying it is because, so fucking what? Of course the poor get fucked by the system. The poor have always gotten fucked by the system. But lawyers make money off the poor, too. I'm not saying what you do isn't exemplary, Charlie. I'm *glad* you do it. I'm glad you do what you do for people. I'm just saying that you make money from it, too."

Bell paused and sat back. He then moved his chair forward with his body, putting his elbows on the table, sitting on the edge of his chair. "I can't remember if I told you," he said to Morand, "about my leukemia?"

"Your leukemia?" Morand said with a puzzled look.

"I have leukemia," Bell said. "Chronic lymphocytic leukemia."

"No," Morand said. "You didn't tell me. When did this happen?"

"A year ago. When was the last time we talked? It must have been over a year ago."

"What precisely," Morand asked slowly, "is chronic leukemia?"

"You've never had a chronic-leukemia disability case? I may need to hire you," Bell said with a laugh. "It's cancer of the bone marrow. The doctors call it the good leukemia. The bad kind—you're dead real fast. With this I can live another twenty years, maybe. They've got me on a chemical regimen—that's what they call it, a regimen. It's not too bad, except that I get really tired sometimes."

"How have your partners been about it?" Morand asked.

"All right. What can they say? I'm not billing what some of them are, but I let them have the money. I'm still paying my way. The big worry is what they call a blastic phase. It's O.K. for a while. Then, without any notice, it's out of control." Bell shrugged. "It doesn't end well—but, finally, it doesn't end well anyway, does it?"

"Are your doctors good?"

"The first one I went to was a sadist. He starts describing what's going to happen to my brain. The doctor I have now I like. The hardest part is that I have two families. My two little ones are only nine and eleven. Janet's twenty-seven now. She's a lawyer, you know."

"I didn't know that. Janet's a lawyer?" said Morand.

"She's with Meyer Lansburgh Doracko & Bartot in Newark. I've had to redo my will. What a mess! No matter what you decide to do, there are problems—someone's unhappy. Funny how everyone despises the lawyers, but everyone loves their money. Including other lawyers. You know, there's a high percentage of disease showing up among lawyers our age. If someone were to do a study, the statistics, I'd bet, would be alarming."

"I have a friend who got pancreatic cancer," said Morand. "Dead in six months."

"Pancreatic cancer! I know of, let's see"—Bell counted off on his fingers—"one, two, three, four, five. Five instances of lawyers who died of pancreatic cancer. I mentioned the fact to my doctor—this is the doctor I like. She says—she puts her head back and gives me this impish smile. 'Well,' she said, 'when you consider what lawyers secrete, that doesn't surprise me.' Hah, hah, hah. You know what else she told me?

A lot of young lawyers are on Prozac. Do you know what Prozac does?"

"I have clients on it," Morand said.

"It affects the same part of the brain LSD does. It's as though you were having a chronic low LSD buzz."

"So that's what explains some of my clients' more exotic behavior," Morand said.

"A partner of mine"—Bell went on—"they discovered a tumor in his brain, they told him it was benign. He quit. Retired at forty-eight. Checked out. He lives up in Vermont near the Canadian border. It's the goddamn investment bankers. They've fucked it all up. They have to be out at forty-five—they're all into how much you need to retire. For thirty to forty years. Ten million, minimum, is the going rate —that's the last figure I heard. Ten million cash! As if there isn't already enough to make you crazy."

"It's what law can't touch," Morand said.

"What? Cancer?" Bell asked.

"The feeling in each one of us—to be in perfect union with another human being. The only thing, finally, that has any real meaning."

"Perfect union?" Bell asked. "Like, 'we the People of the United States, in order to form a more perfect union'?"

"I'm serious," Morand said.

"I'm not sure what you mean," Bell said. "You mean the right to be left alone?"

"No. Not everyone wants to be left alone. I mean what's inside every human being. The desire to be perfectly at one with another human being. It's what law has nothing to do with. It's the only thing—the only thing—that has nothing, absolutely nothing, to do with law.''

Bell and Morand left a few minutes before Keri Egan, my cousin's friend, arrived. After apologizing for being late, she sat down, then stood up again, took her cream-colored suit jacket off, then folded it lengthwise, placing it carefully on the seat of an empty chair. She had on a blue silk blouse, a pearl necklace, and studded pearl earrings. Slender, with blue eyes and shoulder-length black hair, she spoke quickly and energetically, yet with a certain reticence. ''I don't have much time,'' she said, ordering a bottle of Amstel. We spoke briefly about my cousin Marilyn. ''But,'' she said, ''you want to hear what I think about law, right?'' I nodded. ''Perhaps I'm not the right person to be asking,'' she said, sitting upright in her chair, her hands flat on the table. ''I'm in the process of looking for a job.'' I asked her about Daley Pincus and she said that she'd been told to leave. ''All but one person in my class has,'' she said. ''It's been that way for at least two years, but what was tacit is now *very* explicit.'' I asked if she was looking for another firm. ''I'd like to go in-house,'' she said, ''but I'm flexible. I'm thinking of moving to California. Perhaps Warner Brothers. I don't know.'' The tone of her voice changed. ''You know, I saw this incredible scene in the Fulton Market before I came here. A song was playing on the speaker system—the words were something like, 'Everything's out of control, so hold onto your hat, hold onto your soul.' There was this darling little girl—nine or ten years old—standing beside her mother, listening to the words. She didn't think anyone was watching. After she heard the words, she put one hand over her heart, the other on her head, like she was holding onto her hat! Don't you think that's weird?''

The waitress brought Egan her beer. She took a sip and then relaxed her shoulders, sitting back in her chair and listening to the band for a while. "Daley Pincus really sucks,'' she said. ''I can hardly walk in the place anymore. Everyone talking in their low, monotone voices. If you raise your voice you're looked at like you're a deviant, the noise level is so controlled—while you know that there are people walking around with their insides ready to *explode*. There's this one partner I've had to do a lot of work for. He's forty. Right after he became partner he married this mousy paralegal. He speaks in this soft, kind of faggy voice—he thinks he's this stud, a sensitive stud. It's incredible. You have to sit there and listen to him talk about himself, he's always telling— he calls them his war stories. Like what he does is like war. You have to smile and pay attention to him—he gets very upset if you don't. His specialty is NAFTA, so he's always talking about who he knows in Washington, he drops all these names, he's so impressed with himself. He travels all the time to Mexico—he'll go on and on about how much he knows about Mexican art. Well, *I* know something about Mexican art, and he doesn't know anything. He thinks he's this big-deal partner, but the really smart partners think he's a second-rater. The partners who run the firm are too busy to bother with their egos—they just work. A lot of people want to get out, you know."

"Out of law?" I asked.

"Absolutely," said Egan. "A high percentage of the people I know—if they could—would get out. My theory is that there are a lot of lawyers who are lawyers because there was nothing else you could be. I wasn't about to tell my parents I wanted to teach high school. No one hates lawyers to the extent that they want their child *not* to be one. If you don't like math or science, if you're not into computers, if you don't want to go the M.B.A. route—which I think is worse than law school—what do you do? If you're verbal, you go to law school. If you *don't*—especially if you don't even consider it—there's something wrong with you. My friends from Northwestern who didn't go to law school—Marilyn's an architect, so I don't have any trouble with her—have this *incredible* defensiveness about it. I know so many things they don't. M.B.A.s—M.B.A.s really don't know what goes on. It's the age of lawyers—you *have* to be a lawyer. Has it been worth the time and the money? Law school was such a joke! I hated it."

Egan took another sip of beer. "You know," she said after a while, "I work only a few blocks away but never—I think I've been to the Seaport twice. Where," she asked, "is Chinatown from here?"

I said that Water Street merged with Pearl Street and that Chinatown was up Pearl, past the Brooklyn Bridge.

"I love Chinatown," she said. "I have a friend who practices there."

"In Chinatown?" I asked.

"In a high-rise on the main strip there—I think it's Bowery Street. She works out of her apartment. She's made it into an office. Real high-tech. The works. Writes everything off."

"Are her clients Chinese?" I asked.

"She's very interesting," said Egan. "I met her through a friend of mine who's a publicist. They're both from Oregon—Portland, Oregon. The lawyer's Irish. Irish Irish. Her parents came over in the seventies from Ireland. From Northern Ireland. She is *reeeeea*lly intense—I mean *innnnn*-tense!"

I asked again if her clients were Chinese.

"I'm sure they are. But I really don't know to what extent. I know she does some immigration. I've always thought immigration would be fascinating. Annie—that's the Irish Irish girl's name—talked about how, sometimes, when she needs to see a client, she gets taken through these tunnels that go between some of the buildings. I hear, in immigration cases, you get a lump sum—Annie didn't tell me this. Someone else I know who knows someone who does it told me—you get, like, five thousand up front for the whole citizenship thing, from start to finish. You can make a lot of money that way, except I know I'd get bored too quickly. I have a good friend who's with Landau Wyman—you know, the divorce firm, on Madison in the Thirties. With divorce you get paid up front, but you can keep the clock running, too. People who go through a divorce need someone to talk to, and they like to talk to their lawyers—that's what my friend says. She says that, at a certain point, even if you tell your client it's already costing her more not

to settle than to settle—when you're basically telling
her she's already paid you too much—she almost always says you're right, and then keeps on paying you!
Lawyers think clients care about them, one way or
the other. Ego, ego! Clients want what they're paying
you for, as cheaply as they can get it, and they're the
ones who determine what they want—it doesn't matter what kind of practice you're in. I'd never do divorce. Who needs being on call twenty-four hours a
day—called in the middle of the night. Even if I could
bill double-time. No way.''

"So your friend in Chinatown . . .''

"She's not really a friend," Egan corrected me.
"More like a friend of a friend. I've met her only
once. She showed us, me and my friend, this statue,
right on the Bowery—a statue of Confucius. There's
a wild—I guess it's a quotation. It's called the Ta
Tung. That's the way it's spelled on the statue—Ta
Tung. According to my boyfriend, the spelling that
you usually see is Da Dung—he thought I was trying
to be funny when I said Ta Tung. Annie says Ta Tung
is how it's spelled in the old translations. It means the
Great Harmony. Annie gave me a card—she's made
a card up with the quotation on it. She does her own
desktop publishing. Here, I have it in my purse.''

Egan rummaged through her purse and pulled out
a folded piece of paper. "Here. I'll just read you part
of it. This is right in Chinatown! On the statue it's all
in caps. WHEN THE GREAT PRINCIPLE PREVAILS THE
WORLD IS A COMMONWEALTH IN WHICH RULERS ARE
SELECTED ACCORDING TO THEIR WISDOM AND ABILITY.
And a bit down. Here. PROVISION IS SECURED TO THE
AGED TILL DEATH EMPLOYMENT FOR THE ABLE BODIED

AND THE MEANS OF GROWING UP FOR THE YOUNG.
There's no punctuation. And this, this is how it
ends—this is really cool. THEY—the rulers—DO NOT
LIKE TO SEE WEALTH LYING IDLE YET THEY DO NOT
KEEP IT FOR THEIR OWN GRATIFICATION THEY DESPISE
INDOLENCE YET THEY DO NOT USE THEIR ENERGIES
FOR THEIR OWN BENEFIT IN THIS WAY SELFISH SCHEM-
INGS ARE REPRESSED AND ROBBERS THIEVES AND
OTHER LAWLESS MEN NO LONGER EXIST AND THERE IS
NO NEED FOR PEOPLE TO SHUT THEIR OUTER DOORS
THIS IS THE GREAT HARMONY. Neat, heh? It's from
the twelve- or thirteen-hundreds.''

"You still haven't told me what her practice is,"
I said.

"Oh, I don't know," Egan half sighed. "My friend
thinks she buys companies and sells them. She sets up
the deals herself. Here and in Asia. You know how
lawyers are when it comes to how they make their
money. She's *very* secretive. My friend says she has
cousins in Ireland who are in the I.R.A., but says
she's not political. She speaks fluent Mandarin *and*
Cantonese. Learned it in college, a small college in
Minnesota, near Minneapolis. Carleton, I think. She's
fluent. I will say this about her—she doesn't put her
degrees on her wall! She's *real* high-tech. She's got
everything she needs. Hewlett-Packard color printer
and copier, mega-hardware. Does everything herself.
She told us a great story. She was on a plane to Seattle
and behind her were a man and a woman who didn't
know each other but started talking to each other—
very loud—and didn't stop the entire trip. They told
each other their life stories. The woman said she was
'in the security business.' Annie, of course, thought

she meant 'security' as in, you know, the Securities and Exchange Act type of security. The man thought so, too—he said he was in the securities business, and started explaining how, recently, he's been buying life insurance policies from HIV-infected persons at reduced value, then selling them to investors who become beneficiaries. The woman laughed and said, 'No, I mean the security security business.' She was in the robot business—robots who deliver warnings to people entering office complexes. She was a sales rep. Annie said—and this is my point—that there *she* was, on her way to buy a bank, and she realized that you can't buy or sell a bank without a lawyer. She thought to herself, someone who sells robots for a robot manufacturer, or the life insurance policies of people who have AIDS—*anyone* who buys or sells *anything*, anything at all—boxing gloves, boxer dogs —has to have a lawyer. Everyone who buys or sells anything has—someone, some firm, somewhere—a lawyer. No wonder there are so many lawyers!''

Egan interrupted herself. ''*That's* what I wanted to say!'' she said. ''I was by myself on the elevator in the Met Life building—on my way to lunch at the City Club. There were these two lawyers, men, mid-to-late thirties, from Robinson & Froth—their offices are on the twenty-fifth to twenty-eighth floors. We were the only ones on the elevator. The one says to the other, 'I'm fighting a t.r.o.—the crybabies are complaining about their water being poisoned! Poor ba-bies! Boo-hoo-hoo-hoo-hoo.' He's got, you know, that kind of look in his eyes—you know, he doesn't care what you think and wants you to know it. He wouldn't have known that I was a lawyer, but even if he did, it wouldn't have made any difference. He *wanted* me to hear what he was saying. Oink-oink-oink-oink-oink! A pig! Oink-oink-oink-oink-oink!''

Egan asked for the check. ''I'll get it,'' she said. She took an American Express Gold Card from her purse, then glanced at her watch. She turned in her chair and looked toward the East River, and then turned back. ''There's this associate at Daley Pincus,'' she said, her eyes following the hostess walking a young man and woman to another table. ''He's the only one of the group of us who started together who's still on-track. He's not really a bad person,'' she said, looking directly at me again. ''He's going to make partner. He went to N.Y.U. and dated a friend of mine before he met Elishia—Ay-leesh-ee-ah, that's how he says it. The love of his life, Ay-leesh-ee-ah. When we were first-year associates he brought me a cassette of songs he wrote and sang when he was in law school. He told me that he wrote songs, but asked me not to tell anyone. Last week he came up to me— he was worried I'd told, or might tell, someone about it now that word is out I'm definitely off-track. My boyfriend, you know—two years at Simon & Skidmore and that was enough. He was born in the Ukraine. He's a genius. He came over here when he was twelve, hardly spoke a word of English. Thirteen years later, he's graduated from Columbia Law School. He says that the value of being a lawyer is that you don't have to deal with the lawyers—unless it's on *your* terms. He does joint ventures—out of New York, although we're thinking of L.A. He did a very big deal in Hungary. He says that when he starts talking American law over there—it doesn't matter what, he says, just the fact that you can talk the talk—there's this hush. The Hungarians, he says, start hitting the bottle. They're terrified of American lawyers. *Petrified.* Even the mafia. No matter where in the world, my boyfriend says—you have to deal with American lawyers. He loves it.''

The waitress brought Egan her credit card and the check. She signed it and put the card back in her wallet, and then her wallet into her purse. "Give Marilyn my best," she said. "You know," she continued, standing up to put her suit jacket on, then sitting down again, "when you said you wanted to talk about law, I remembered . . . My boyfriend has a friend—a girl he met through a Ukrainian friend of his. She's our age. *Extraordinarily* beautiful. Her eyes are violet blue. Slightly slanted—Slavic-like, you know? She's blond, strawberry blond. She was born in St. Louis. Her mother's Czech. She's—well, she was an actress. She couldn't handle the business— what you've got to go through to be an actress, just couldn't do it. Her father was a shoe salesman or something. Very—kind of hypersensitive. Dropped out sophomore year from some small college in Pennsylvania. She's had all sorts of lovers. Men—some very educated and rich—fall in love just looking at her, she's that beautiful. She worked for years as a waitress. She does word processing now. She prefers working as a temp. No health insurance, nothing like that—I don't know what she would do if she had to go into the hospital. She's worked at some law firms —she worked night shift for a while at Brownwell & Eliot. Imagine her at Brownwell & Eliot!"

"Why not?"

"Why not? I don't know! She's so small and Brownwell & Eliot is so big! Her being around all that money, the power plays, the"—Egan snapped her fingers—"go-go-go-go-go. She . . . She's, like, the kind of person who suddenly will start talking about reconnecting her spirit to her body. Those aren't the kind of connections people at Brownwell & Eliot are particularly interested in! She hardly ever reads the newspaper. I don't think Melissa—her name's Melissa—I don't think she even owns a TV. Movies, yes—she likes movies, foreign films. She listens to all kinds of music. She reads. She loves to read. Marguerite Duras. Robert Frost. She loves Robert Frost. She's the kind of person who really can't understand how there can be war—she's incapable of comprehending how it can even happen. You're sitting there talking about Chechnya or someplace like that, and she says she can't understand why it's happening. Anyhow, there we are, my boyfriend and me, both of us lawyers, so one day I ask her what she thinks about lawyers. She answers by getting into a long story about a boyfriend of a friend of hers who tested positive for marijuana and was fired from his job—he was a commodities trader, the kind who's only been to college. My boyfriend responded by saying, 'Well, that makes sense.' Melissa looked at him and asked him why it made sense. 'He's not worth the capitation,' my boyfriend said. Melissa had this look of horror on her face! 'What do you mean, capitation?'—she was very angry. 'You know,' my boyfriend said, 'you fire him because of what he might cost you because he smokes grass and you can hire someone for the job who doesn't.' My boyfriend

didn't realize until later—decapitate. He was fired—
they cut his head off. Those were the connections Melissa was making. Well, after that, she got very quiet.
Then she started coming up with all these things about
lawyers."

There was a sudden gust of wind, papers from a
nearby table caught up in it, a few of which swirled
around our table. We reached to try to catch them,
and managed to grab a couple. Egan took them over
to the woman at the nearby table, then sat down
again. "Melissa," she said, "said that lawyers always
seemed to be saying something other than what they
meant."

"That lawyers are manipulative?" I asked.

"No. It was different than that. She said that lawyers have large shadows. Anything light, she said,
makes their shadows even larger. She put her thumb
and index finger together, in the form of a circle.
'Lawyers are like this,' she said, placing her right
index finger into the circle, 'like this,' she said, slowly
drawing it out."

MacKnight Was Murdered

CITY PRIMEVAL—IT'S SUBTITLED *HIGH NOON IN Detroit*. One of Elmore Leonard's best. It opens with a judge whose name is Guy—Judge Guy. A judge on Detroit's criminal court—Recorder's Court. The state Judicial Tenure Commission is recommending his disbarment for all sorts of niceties—sexually soliciting defense counsel while on the bench, abusing counsel, litigants, court personnel, spectators, even newspaper reporters. He's leaving a suburban racetrack with a woman. He's around fifty, she's in her late twenties—a call-girl maybe, it's not clear. While on an altogether different track there's—Clement's his name, a bona fide killer, who's following an Albanian he wants to rob. The Albanian's supposed to have a pile of money hidden in a safe in a secret room in his basement. Clement tries to cut in front of Guy so as not to lose the Albanian, but Guy won't let him, so Clement ends up losing the Albanian and is pissed off—we're talking psychopathically pissed off. Clement then follows Guy's Continental Mark IV onto the interstate highway, puts the front bumper of his car —literally bumps it—against the back of Guy's, they're both going sixty, seventy miles an hour. Guy veers off onto an exit, Clement manages to follow, Guy has the girl dial 911 on the car phone, pulls into the parking lot of a tool-and-die shop—remember, this is Detroit. Clement gets out of his car and shoots the judge five times through the windshield with a Walther P.38 automatic. He ends up killing the girl, too. There's a passage in one of the early chapters, where one of the detectives asks another detective about suspects—who might have had a reason to kill His Honor. He then says something like, 'Give me a paper and pencil and a month, that's how many names we're talking about.' Conservatively, he figures, twenty-six hundred names, right off the bat— the number of people Guy may have rubbed the wrong way—defense lawyers, cops, prosecutors, everyone he'd ever sent to prison, everyone he'd ever abused, which was almost everyone he'd ever come in contact with. There's another line, something like, 'Every man or woman who ever knew him, it went through their minds at one time or other to kill him.' There was a real Recorder's Court judge at the time —the Tenure Commission had recommended his disbarment. He appealed to the Michigan Supreme Court. His appeal was before the Court when I was clerking for one of the justices.''

Stan Ayres interrupted me. ''I've got to make a

phone call," he said. We'd just finished lunch at the
Bridge Café, on Water Street near the Brooklyn
Bridge. "Now if this were L.A., I'd just snap my cell
out. But this is New York. When in New York, use a
pay phone," he said, getting up and walking over to
a pay phone behind the bar. Ayres and I had been
associates at the same firm in the early eighties. He
began working there right out of Columbia Law
School. He left New York City in eighty-eight, to practice with a large firm in Los Angeles, made partner,
and then, in ninety-three, left with several other partners to join another, smaller firm. Now in his late
thirties, he'd put on some weight—he'd always been
trim—but, as usual, he still exuded a world-weary
savoir-faire. He'd grown his light brown hair long,
especially in back. His eyes were round and a blue-
gray. Dressed casually in light khakis and a dark blue
shirt and loafers, he was visiting New York City for
a week, on vacation. His practice was mostly—he
filled me in—various kinds of legal work for two small
pharmaceutical companies. He also represented his
wife's uncle, an investment banker, "a very influen-
tial behind-the-scenes telecommunications mogul, in
fact. So," he added, "I hobnob with stars." I asked
if he knew any of the "trash for cash" bar.

He laughed. "How about the 'your cash ain't
nothing but trash' bar?"

He returned to the table after making his call, sat
down, then shook his head. I asked if anything was
the matter. "Even if there was," he said, "there's
nothing I can do about it." We'd finished eating and
had ordered coffee. It was a moist, clear late-August
day. The restaurant was flooded with light. Through

its windows facing Dover Street, one could see the Brooklyn Bridge. "I thought of you the other day," said Ayres. "A friend of mine represents a small bank. Some crazo takes a track loader—like, a bulldozer—from a construction site near the bank and rams it—you know, the metal teeth on the blade—right through the wall of the bank, then scoops out the broken glass, the bricks from the wall, and, of course, the night-deposit box. The bank's insured, but wants to know if it can sue the construction company."

"I don't know," I said. "You've got the advantage of hindsight. The fact that it happened. If someone had been more careful—if there'd been a security guard, for example—maybe it wouldn't have. You probably have enough to get to a jury."

"Isn't there an intervening-cause issue?"

"You can get past it by arguing that it was a foreseeable intervening cause. The construction company should have foreseen that someone might steal a track loader and then cause injury—it should have taken adequate precautions to prevent it. You don't have to foresee a crazo ramming a track loader into a bank, just someone stealing it and causing injury. The construction company's going to argue that no reasonable person would have foreseen the type of injury that occurred—property loss, the money stolen from the night-deposit box. How much, by the way, was stolen?"

"A hundred thousand and change."

"The construction company's going to say that the most a reasonable person would have foreseen is someone stealing a track loader and getting into an accident with, let's say, a car."

"What if," Ayres asked, "the construction company is a subcontractor?"

"And you want to sue the contractor?" I asked. "Problems. I'd have to know more facts."

"Man, I don't know how anybody does that kind of thing."

"What? Ram a loader into a bank?"

"That," Ayres said, "I can understand. I mean figure out subcontractor liability. Give me the plain and the simple."

"So," I asked, "what have you been doing that's so plain and simple?"

"Just trying to unwind several transactions between a client of mine—a former Kazakh general-turned-entrepreneur. At least he tells me he's a Kazakh. One of his colleagues told me he's really Kirghiz—Kirghizstan, as you no doubt don't know, is between Kazakhstan and China. Just the other side of the Transcaucasus."

"You've got to be kidding."

Ayres smiled. "You're right. I am. I'm just making it up. I have nothing to do with Transtranscaucasians. I'm a domestic fellow. Liens. Liens and cease-and-desist orders. I have nothing to do with liens and cease-and-desist orders, either—but, at least, it's closer to home. I don't know if you have any of these hate-the-government militia here, but, out where I live, we do. Slapping liens on the government officials who prosecute them for things like embezzlement and tax fraud. The government gets a cease-and-desist order, so they slap a lien on the government lawyers whose names are on the order, then send it back stamped REFUSED FOR CAUSE WITHOUT DISHONOR U.C.C. 3-501—having scrupulously studied the Uniform Commercial Code, article three, section five-o-one. They even sell software—'how-to-fuck-the federal-government-with-the-U.C.C.' software! You don't believe me, do you? It so happens as we speak. Here you are, an Assistant U.S. Attorney, a lien on your ass, your cease-and-desist order stamped by a reference to article three, section five-o-one, of the U.-fucking-C.-C.! Think it might make you reconsider why you've chosen the public sector?''

Ayres finished his coffee and asked the waiter for a Hennessy X.O. ''Nothing like the glow''—he said —''of Hennessy X.O.'' With a nod of the head, he took a sip, then sat back in his chair. ''So,'' he said, ''the *real* judge. There was a real judge.''

''The Recorder's Court judge who appealed his disbarment to the Michigan Supreme Court?''

''Why was he disbarred?''

''I don't want to get into it.''

''What do you mean, you don't want to get into it.''

''That's what I said. I don't want to get into it.''

''When was this?''

''Nineteen seventy-seven.''

''What did the Court do?''

''The Court upheld the Tenure Commission's recommendation. The real judge was disbarred.''

''Why?''

''I don't want to get into it,'' I said again. ''I've always wondered, though, what Leonard knew. He'd hang around the Frank Murphy Hall of Justice, which is across Beaubien Street from Police Headquarters. About half a mile from where I clerked in the old Lafayette Building, between Lafayette Street and Michigan Avenue, across the street from the federal courthouse—downtown Detroit.''

"The Frank Murphy Hall of Justice?''

"It's Recorder's Court. Murphy was a Recorder's Court judge in the twenties—before he was Mayor of Detroit, Governor of Michigan, Governor General of the Philippines, Attorney General of the United States, and then an Associate Justice of the United States Supreme Court. There was, though, another— I guess you could call it interesting—appeal around the same time the real judge was appealing, which I could say something about.''

"Another appeal?'' asked Ayres.

"An unrelated appeal,'' I said.

"Tell me about it,'' Ayres said.

"The long or the short version?''

"Any version you want. I'm on vacation.''

"Well,'' I said, "I should probably begin with MacKnight.''

"MacKnight?''

"Raymond Thomas 'Mack' MacKnight, Junior. Ray MacKnight. We went to high school together. The University of Detroit High School—the Jesuit high school in Detroit. We were there back in the early sixties. Sixty-two to sixty-six. Out of a thousand students there were twenty, thirty black kids, at most.''

"MacKnight was black?''

"MacKnight was black. He used to insist 'Mack' be spelled with a 'k,' like in Mack Avenue, which is this very tough street that cuts across Detroit's lower east side. There was a Chrysler factory—Mack Stamping. A massive stamping plant. *Mack the Knife*, too—the Bobby Darin song—was a hit when we were in eighth grade. It was Mack's song. MacKnight was a good athlete—very good, in fact. Basketball especially. He was big—six-seven by the time we were seniors. Detroit was segregated, like every large city in America at the time. One school, Catholic Central—there was a big game when we were freshmen, held in the University of Detroit's Memorial Building. MacKnight was one of two or three freshmen on the reserve team. During the reserve game—before the varsity game, which was for the championship—the Catholic Central kids kept calling MacKnight nigger. He was the only black kid on either team, reserve or varsity. There was a crowd of five thousand high school kids, almost all white. Everyone knew what was happening. Things got so hot that the Jesuit coaching our team didn't stop our players from an all-out fistfight. The game had to be stopped, the police had to stop the stands from emptying. Our junior year, the state tournament, there was a game at our gym, Highland Park versus Southwestern. There were stabbings after the game. The next round of games was played without spectators. It was a big thing, in the newspapers and everything. This was before there were guns everywhere—the guns and drugs came in two years later, with the riots and with Vietnam. MacKnight had a definite visibility—All-Catholic, All-State. He was a good student, too."

"Were you friends?"

"We'd say hello—that was about it. My uncle and

my dad owned a small bodega-type liquor and grocery store on what was then the most violent strip in the city—there's a store on the corner of One Twenty-fifth and Madison that looks just like it. MacKnight told my cousin the price that my uncle charged for bananas was too high—your father, in effect, is a usurper. This was when we were seniors. MacKnight, apparently, had gone into the store, or he was just getting in my cousin's face—who knows? I don't remember my cousin hating him, or MacKnight hating my cousin. It never got anywhere near that. It was more like everyone had to let everyone else know his place. In our senior year, the second game of the state tournament, we played the number-one-ranked team in the state, Hamtramck High. Hamtramck was mostly black, except for its center, Rudy Tomjanovich."

"The coach of the Rockets?"

"Do you think there are two Rudy Tomjanoviches? We won. MacKnight covered Tomjanovich man-to-man and outplayed him. Don't get me wrong. MacKnight played the best game of his life and Tomjanovich still scored over twenty points, and, at the end of the game, made—I'll never forget it—three perfect jump shots from twenty-five feet out. If you were to ask Tomjanovich today if he remembered MacKnight, I'm sure he would. He'd admit, too, that MacKnight outplayed him—I'm sure he remembers everyone who's ever outplayed him. Everyone from Hamtramck remembers everything."

"Wasn't Tomjanovich involved in a suit against Kermit Washington?"

"That's right. I forgot about that. In the seventies. Washington punched him in the face during a free-for-all. Tomjanovich sued the Lakers. Negligent supervision."

"Negligent supervision? Why not battery?"

"The Lakers would have argued that Washington was outside the scope of his employment. Tomjanovich could have sued Washington for battery—I'm sure there was money there—but I don't think he did. I remember reading that the doctor who testified for Tomjanovich said his face had to be put back together like a jigsaw puzzle. Tomjanovich won three million dollars in federal district court. The Lakers appealed—Tomjanovich settled. It became an important case in insurance circles. They stopped underwriting—at least for a while—'participant-to-participant' sports liability coverage. If your player lost it and you got sued, you paid. I'm sure now there are intricate indemnification agreements between the players and the teams. The biggest impact it had was on hockey. They changed the rules."

The waiter asked if we were interested in dessert, pointing to a small blackboard where the day's specials were written in chalk. We said no. Ayres asked for another Hennessy X.O. The sun in his eyes, he moved his chair a few feet to the side. "Did Mac-Knight," he asked, "play ball in college?"

"He went to Eastern Michigan, in Ypsilanti—known as Ypsi-tucky by the locals—on a basketball scholarship. I was a few miles away, in Ann Arbor. I never saw him again after high school. I didn't hear about him again until May of seventy-one. I was in Cambridge, England—Cambridge University—on a fellowship, studying English."

"How'd you get out of the draft?" Ayres asked.

"A high lottery number," I said. "Three twenty-three. It was the end of the first of two years there. I got a letter from a high school classmate. MacKnight was murdered."

"Murdered?"

"Found murdered on the floor of an apartment in Detroit. No one seemed to know what really happened. My friend wrote that there was a rumor MacKnight was working undercover for the police, another that he was involved in serious radical politics at Wayne State, which is not far from my uncle and father's store—which, by that time, was in real bad shape. It had been burned in sixty-seven in the riots. My father had gotten shot in a robbery by a heroin addict when I was a senior in college. My father was working—in addition to four nights a week at the store—a full-time job as a meat cutter with A & P. My uncle sold the store a few months later, in early April seventy-two. I remember my mother's letter. I was in Strasbourg—in a café across from the Cathedral. My uncle sold it for almost nothing. He was how old, my uncle, when he sold the store? Fifty-six. My father was fifty-four. My uncle went to work for Dodge Truck, on the assembly line. Later, spring of seventy-two, I was still in Cambridge—I got another letter, from the same classmate. A small poetry press in Detroit, which published only black poets, posthumously published a book of poems by MacKnight."

"A book of poems?"

"My friend sent it to me. MacKnight apparently had been writing poems back when he was in high

school. There's a photograph of Mack at a demon-
stration—leather coat, sideburns, Afro, this intense,
serious look on his face—on the back of the book. It
cost a dollar twenty-five.''

"Is it any good?''

"He was twenty-two years old.''

Ayres moved his body around in his chair. He was
shaking his head.

"Do you want me to stop?'' I asked.

"No, go on,'' Ayres said, then paused. "Did you
find out how he died?''

"I finished at Cambridge in seventy-two and returned to Detroit late that year. I began law school
—I was a summer starter—in Ann Arbor, May
seventy-three. Before that, I worked a few months in
the factory. I was—obsessed is too strong a word. I
wanted to know what really happened. I'd see someone who'd known MacKnight and ask what he'd
heard. The same answers—MacKnight was into radical politics, he was working undercover for the police. No one really knew. After law school—this is
May of seventy-six—my first job is a two-year clerkship with the Michigan Supreme Court. Not even a
year into the clerkship, sometime in early seventy-
seven, I get a call from another justice's clerk. He'd
gone to Brother Rice High School, one of the other
Detroit-area all-boys Catholic high schools. He was a
couple of years younger than I was, but, like everyone
who ever saw him, he remembered MacKnight. He
asked me if I'd seen the Commissioner's Report on
MacKnight's murder.''

Ayres looked puzzled.

"A Commissioner's Report—we called them CR's," I said. "They're Supreme Court staff memos recommending, or not recommending, leaves to appeal. First the clerks, and then the justices, read them. There was one concerning—I guess that's what you could say it was, concerning. Concerning Mac-Knight. A CR concerning the murder of MacKnight."

"Let me get this straight," Ayres said. "There's a report—a memo from a Supreme Court staff attorney of an appeal. By whom? Who's appealing?"

"The person who murdered MacKnight."

"The murderer is appealing?"

"*In propria personae*. It's an *in pro per* appeal by the person who murdered MacKnight. He's in Jackson Prison, the state penitentiary—Michigan's Folsom or Attica. He's been convicted of first-degree murder. Life imprisonment. For the murder of Mac-Knight."

Ayres was shaking his head again.

"I wanted to know how MacKnight died? Well, here! You got it! Right on my desk! I ordered the entire record—five thousand pages. I remember—I came in on a Saturday and a Sunday. It was late March, early April. Both days, I remember, were overcast, gray. I read the whole thing."

"All of it?"

"Some parts more closely than others. You know, it's testimony. Once you get into it, you can read it fast. I wanted to know what happened? Well, I found out."

"This guy killed him?"

"I can tell you what the record says. I made copies of parts of it. I've kept them in a file."

"Goddamn weird!" Ayres said.

"You said you wanted to hear it."

"I know I said I wanted to hear it. Go ahead. I want to hear it."

"The People's primary witness . . ." I paused a few seconds to get my thoughts in order. "The witness for the state is a small-time, street-level drug dealer. Cocaine. Marijuana. His name is Nathaniel. He lives in an apartment on Boston Boulevard, which, in the early part of the century, was a very fashionable street—Henry Ford had a house on Boston Boulevard. The apartment's not far from Aretha Franklin's father's church—the New Bethel Baptist Church. Nathaniel lives with a woman named Audrey, who, he says, disapproves of his dealing drugs—she's terrified of the possible violence. Nathaniel knew MacKnight when they were kids. They grew up in the same neighborhood. He says that, a few weeks before MacKnight was killed, he ran into a woman, Betty, whom he hadn't seen since high school, in a bar near Tiger Stadium. La Players Bar. Betty introduced him to her boyfriend, Albert."

Ayres laughed. "La Players? Sounds French."

"Just past midnight, the thirteenth of April, MacKnight comes over to Nathaniel's apartment. He has two quarters of cocaine, which he wants Nathaniel to sell for him. The prosecutor asks Nathaniel how long he's been dealing. About a year, he says. He started dealing to make extra money so he could attend hairdresser's school."

"He was a beautician?"

"He testifies MacKnight wasn't his partner or anything like that. MacKnight just wanted Nathaniel to sell the cocaine for him. After he sold it, MacKnight would get a cut of what Nathaniel got.''

''MacKnight's not even selling it to him?''

''No. He wants Nathaniel to sell it for him.''

''What's a quarter of cocaine?''

''A tablespoon. It's in the record. We're talking about two tablespoons of cocaine.''

''Do you think MacKnight was dealing?''

''No. He wasn't dealing. There's a line of cross— of MacKnight's father—by one of the defendant's lawyers, about what MacKnight was doing at the time. Here's Mr. MacKnight, a witness for the prosecution. He says that Mack was taking classes at Wayne and teaching some in the Detroit public schools. My guess is he was trying to stay out of the draft—you could get a deferment if you were in graduate school or a teacher. He lived at home, Mr. MacKnight says, but was hardly ever there. His dad—I think his mother had died—ran a gas station, which was located in a heavily Muslim neighborhood. Mack would help him out. Mr. MacKnight says he remembered Nathaniel from when he was a child. There's an opaque line of questioning about whether Mr. MacKnight reads the newspapers—the *Detroit Free Press*, *The Detroit News*—whether he had any conversations with any of Mack's friends about the work his son was doing for the city. Mr. MacKnight said that all he knew was that Mack was working for the Board of Education. There must have been—I don't know—something in the papers about Mack working undercover for the city.''

"Do you think he was?"

"Do you know what I think? I think he came across two tablespoons of cocaine—a hundred dollars' worth, at most. Nathaniel testified he sold it to Albert for a hundred seventy-five. After Nathaniel's cut, what would MacKnight have gotten? That's the level this is going on. MacKnight is working at his dad's gas station to help him out but also to make some money. He's probably getting an education degree from Wayne and is into some heavy activism, the kind that was going around those days. This is three years after King was murdered—four years after the worst civil riot in the history of the United States. Which, I remind you, occurred in Detroit—surpassed only recently by that little eruption out there a couple of years ago where you live, in the City of Angels. There is, in fact, a reference in the record—Mack's father's testimony—about Mack having just come back from L.A. He probably met some woman out there. He probably wanted to get some quick money so he could go back—he was probably in love. Do you know *Laird v. Tatum*? It's a Supreme Court opinion, from right around the time MacKnight was killed. Army Intelligence was spying on political activists in Detroit. I'm sure Mack was on one list or another—they'd gather names from photographs. The photograph on the back of his book of poems was probably in an Army Intelligence file."

"The direct examination," Ayres said. "There was Betty. Betty and what's-his-name . . ."

"Albert. Albert and Betty. They come over to Nathaniel's apartment. Around two in the morning.

"Let me speed this up," I said. "Two in the morning Albert and Betty come over to Nathaniel's apartment to buy cocaine. Audrey is asleep, MacKnight is still there. Albert and Betty sample some cocaine—say they like it—and buy it. They're ready to leave. Nathaniel opens the door to let them out when two men with guns drawn—they're sticking their guns in Nathaniel's face—break into the apartment. Albert's suddenly drawn a gun, too. Betty splits. Nathaniel says to Albert, 'You can have it all.' Albert spins him around, puts his gun to Nathaniel's head, pushes him face down against the floor. One of the others does the same thing with MacKnight. One of them goes into the bedroom and gets Audrey. Audrey, MacKnight, and Nathaniel are lying on the floor, guns to their heads. Albert pulls Nathaniel up—he says that he wants his drugs, diamonds, money.''

"Diamonds?''

"It's in the record. For some reason or other, Albert thinks Nathaniel has diamonds. Nathaniel says he only has about a hundred dollars in cash and some cocaine—that's it. Albert pushes Nathaniel back on the floor. He tells Audrey to get up. Someone takes Audrey into the bedroom. A gun goes off.''

"My God,'' Ayres said.

"The prosecutor asks Nathaniel to tell him what happened then. Nathaniel says, 'Ray MacKnight—he asks what's going on. He's trying to get up, you know—he's saying he's got nothing to do with this. He's just trying to get by—he's got nothing to do with this! He's got nothing to do with this!' Albert—Nathaniel says—puts a pillow to MacKnight's head to muffle the sound, and shoots.''

"Incredible.''

"Nathaniel says he knows he's next in line. He tells Albert he's got four thousand dollars in cash in the basement of the apartment building. Albert says he's lying. Albert puts his gun to Nathaniel's head, as he's pushing him against the floor, and fires."

"Fuck," Ayres said, shaking his head. "Incredible."

"You're not wondering," I asked, "how it is—if Nathaniel is shot in the head—he's testifying?"

"You're right," Ayres said. "You mean, he didn't die? How could he not die?"

"Albert put his gun to the side of Nathaniel's head, but—Nathaniel's exact words—'I just got twelve stitches.'"

"Twelve stitches?"

"The prosecutor says—you can see him asking in the kind of voice you can use on direct when you know what you have—'Now, that morning, Nathaniel, were you wearing your hair differently than you are today?' 'Yes, sir,' Nathaniel says. 'Yes, I was.' 'How, on that morning, were you wearing your hair?' 'Well, sir, you see, I had a very large Afro back then.' 'A very large Afro?' 'Yes, sir, a very large Afro.' 'How large was this Afro?' 'Well, sir, it was about as big an Afro as any you'd see.'"

"No!" said Ayres.

"'What happened after you were shot, Nathaniel?' 'I played dead, sir.'"

"Unbelievable."

"There's more," I said. "We're not done yet. Albert and friends ransack the apartment and then split. Audrey's dead. MacKnight is still breathing.

Nathaniel calls the police. He goes with MacKnight to Henry Ford Hospital. Mack dies around six in the morning. I made a copy of the testimony of the doctor who performed the autopsy. He said that the bullet completely fractured MacKnight's skull. 'Additionally,' he said, 'the gentleman had a big heart. His heart weighed five hundred grams.' A gunshot wound to the head and a large heart—MacKnight had a large heart. The doctor was asked to identify Mack's age. 'The gentleman,' he said, 'was twenty-two years old.' Then there's Mack's father's testimony. The prosecutor asked him whose body it was. 'The body of Raymond MacKnight, Junior,' he said. 'Who, sir, was Raymond MacKnight, Junior, in relation to you?' 'My baby son,' Mr. MacKnight said. 'That's my baby son.' "

"Let's get out of here," Ayres said. "Go for a walk."

"We're not finished yet," I said. "We've still got the trial."

"Let's get out of here." We left, walking on Water Street toward Peck Slip. Sea gulls were circling above piles of fish garbage from the Seaport.

"Do you think it's true," I asked, "that New York, compared to L.A., is Old World?"

"What you see in L.A. today is what you'll see in New York tomorrow," said Ayres.

"There was a saying when I was growing up in Detroit," I said. 'As Detroit goes, so goes the nation.' "

"The nation? As L.A. goes, so goes the world."

We crossed Front Street, stopping beneath the

FDR Drive. There were two police vans there. "Why all the police?" Ayres asked. "The Fulton Market," I said. "The city took it over."

"Why?"

"Racketeering."

"Federal court?"

"No. The city's taken over as landlord. It apparently has the power to do so. It's refusing to lease to certain parties. There was a huge fire—the main building in the Market burned to the ground. The city says it was arson."

We continued along the river, passing a four-masted sailing barque, the *Peking*, moored to a pier, toward the tip of the island. I asked Ayres how he felt about being a lawyer. He shrugged. "It's a way to make a living," he said. "It's like any other business. The problem is, most lawyers aren't good businessmen—it's a real problem. We're part of the business world, which is really changing—you either adapt or you don't."

I asked him if he thought it's always been like this. "What are you asking?" he said. "If I think it used to be more of a profession?" "Do you think it was?" I asked. "Who knows?" he said. "How do I know, fifty years ago, if it was any less of a business? What difference does it make if it was? America fifty years ago was like a developing country is today. There are days I feel like I'm a professional. I do what my client needs done, I save him money. I'm not paid to make the laws—I'm paid to figure them out, to make, or to save, my clients money. Some days I feel like I'm a mechanic, other days I take the afternoon off and play golf—I've started playing a lot more golf lately.

It could be worse. The amount of law I deal with, day-in, day-out, compared to the total amount of law there is in this society—it's nothing. What if you're not a lawyer—we can't even imagine anymore what it's like to look at what we look at every day without thinking the way we do. It's impossible. Who was it who said politicians can keep two completely contradictory things in their heads at the same time? Two! I know lawyers who can keep fifty or sixty in their head, actively, yet talk as if there's no contradiction at all. There's this ridiculous, pompous idiot—guy's got more money, much of it questionably obtained, than he can keep track of. A partner at Tally Viereck. He's on TV saying how lawyers used to be our civic leaders, but look at them now. Well, lawyers still *are* our civic leaders. It's just that now our politicians can keep fifty completely contradictory statements in their heads at the same time. Imagine you're not a lawyer and you're listening to this fool—you've got to be thinking, that's the whole point, fuck-face. Lawyers *are* our civic leaders!"

We came to Battery Park and sat on a bench facing the harbor. "You know, the East River is an estuary—a saltwater estuary—not a river. That's what I love about it down here," Ayres said. "It's the sea. You can feel the salt in the air right now."

We sat a few moments in silence. "So," Ayres said, "the trial."

"People v. Albert," I said, "and the other two gunmen."

"Albert for murder one. The other two, I assume, for felony murder, right?"

"Exactly. All three convicted—life in Jackson. A

round of appeals, all denied. Then Albert appeals *in pro per* to the Michigan Supreme Court. But there's one big change in the interim. The Court, in seventy-five, decides a case, *People v. Reed. Reed* says that in a criminal trial, once a plea of not guilty is entered, the defendant has a constitutional right to a jury determination of all the essential elements of the offense. The trial judge in *Reed*—a Recorder's Court judge, it so happens—told the jury that a murder had taken place. The Supreme Court said this assumed an essential element of the crime of murder—the fact that a murder occurred is a part of what the prosecution has to prove. The Court held that unless the defendant expressly agreed to the instruction, it was reversible error. The justice I was clerking for wrote *Reed.* Albert reads it in Jackson. He then reads the transcript of his trial. What's he see, in plain, unequivocal language? The judge telling the jury she's not going to get into the elements of the crime because there's an agreement among all the parties that there was a robbery committed and that in the accomplishment of the robbery Raymond MacKnight was murdered. The only issue left, she says, is who did it.''

"A violation of *People v. Reed*,'' said Ayres.

"Clearly. The judge didn't understand felony murder. What she should have said was that the state had the burden of proving that in the course of a robbery, a felony, a murder was committed by someone who the state must prove committed the murder. If the state meets that burden—which it would have in this case, since the jury believed Nathaniel's testimony that Albert killed MacKnight—then the other two would also be guilty of murder one.''

"That's what happened in the Howard Beach case, isn't it?" asked Ayres.

"It must have. Those who feloniously were chasing the black kid when he was murdered by one of them also committed murder."

"I don't think we even covered felony murder in law school," Ayres said.

"We did. We spent almost half our criminal-law course on it. Our professor—he was a philosopher—it fascinated him. He kept going back into it. I suppose, you could say, Albert did, too. He wrote his own motion, citing *Reed*, appealing directly to the Supreme Court. He says that he never agreed to waive any element of any crime he allegedly committed. Therefore, under *Reed*, the judge's instructions were reversible error. I of course had to stay out of it—I had, you might say, a bit of a conflict. In August seventy-seven, the Court reversed Albert's and the other two defendants' convictions, remanding to Recorder's Court for a new trial."

"Did they retry him?" Ayres asked.

"I had no idea what had happened," I said, "until one day, a couple of years later, right before we moved to New York, the same friend who'd written me in Cambridge about MacKnight's murder calls me on the phone and says there's an article in *The Detroit News* about jailhouse lawyers. Albert is featured."

Ayres laughed. "Of course," he said. "The successful jailhouse lawyer!"

"The other defendants—one asked for a new trial and was acquitted, the other pled to a reduced sentence. So did Albert. All this was in the *News* article.

It doesn't say what Albert pled guilty to. He'd already served nine years, so he was eligible under the reduced plea for parole in a year or so."

"So he was out in a year?" Ayres asked.

"I don't know," I said. "But I did recently go back and reread the parts of the record that I'd copied. I was rereading Nathaniel's testimony. There was something in it I'd missed—or forgotten. The prosecutor is asking Nathaniel about Audrey's wallet. He's trying to establish if there was anything stolen—he's trying to establish a robbery. Robbery's the felony, remember, the basis for the felony murder. The prosecutor—his name is Latkin—asks Nathaniel to tell him what's in the wallet. Nathaniel looks, and says there's nothing in it except a half penny—a penny cut in half in the change purse. The only thing left in Audrey's wallet is half of one cent.

"I told all this once to a federal prosecutor. I've gotten to know Joe Taubman on the Second Circuit —he was appointed last year. He was a district judge for sixteen years before that. When I told him I wanted to talk to lawyers about lawyers and about law, he said I should talk to Rene Coro, who is, Taubman says, in his opinion, one of the most perceptive prosecuting attorneys he's ever seen. So Taubman introduces me to Coro. We have lunch at a Thai restaurant behind the Tombs. I'm telling her this, she seems to be listening, nodding every once in a while, eating slowly. I feel she's watching me, actually watching what I'm saying. The whole time I'm talking, she doesn't say a word. I finish, she moves her half-finished plate of bamboo shoots, bean curd, asparagus, broccoli, shallots, to the side, and she says one thing. 'The Afro.'

"Suddenly she's staring at me with these large, round, cobalt-colored eyes of hers. It was as if she was trying to look through me. 'There are three ways of looking at it,' she said—her voice was soft, but every word distinct. She held her hand up in a fist. 'First,' she said, counting off her thumb, 'what looks large may, in fact, be large. Second'—she put her index finger in the air—'what looks small may not be as small as you think. Third,' she said, counting off a third finger, the slightest trace of a smile on her face, 'what looks large may, in fact, be larger than you think. What looks large may actually be larger than you think!' "